FROM CLAY TO ROCK

CHRISTIAN HERALD BOOKS
Chappaqua, New York

FROM CLAY TO ROCK

**Personal insights
into life from
Simon Peter**

LESLIE B. FLYNN

We acknowledge with appreciation permission to quote from:

"Peter's Confession," by R.V.G. Tasker, © 1957 by CHRISTIANITY TODAY.

Peter: Disciple, Apostle, Martyr, by Oscar Cullman; translated by Floyd V. Filson. Published simultaneously in Great Britain and the U.S.A. by the SCNI Press Ltd., London, and The Westminster Press, Philadelphia, 1953.

HE CAME WITH MUSIC, Moody Press, Chicago, Ill.

"Judas, Peter," by Luci Shaw © 1979 by CHRISTIANITY TODAY.

Acts of the Apostles by G. Campbell Morgan; © 1924 Fleming H. Revell

Library of Congress Cataloging in Publication Data

Flynn, Leslie B.
    Simon Peter, from clay to rock

    1. Peter, Saint, Apostle   2. apostles—
Biography   3 Bible N.T.—Biography.   I. Title.
BS2515.F56   226'.092'4(B)   80—69307
ISBN 0-915684-79-9

First Edition
CHRISTIAN HERALD BOOKS, 40 Overlook Drive, Chappaqua, New York 10514
Printed in the United States of America

MEMBER OF
EVANGELICAL CHRISTIAN
PUBLISHERS ASSOCIATION

Christian Herald, independent, evangelical and interdenominational is dedicated to publishing wholesome, inspirational and religious books for Christian families.

Contents

1. A New Name   9
2. Call to Service   21
3. Walking on Water   33
4. Peter and the Keys   45
5. Glimpse of Glory   57
6. Questions Peter Asked   69
7. Gospel of the Basin   85
8. The Denial   96
9. A New Lease on Life   109
10. The New Peter   121
11. Bulwark to the Brethren   133
12. Under Fire   146

Foreword

Pet rocks were the vogue a few years ago. Nestled in curly wood shavings inside small cardboard carrying cases, the rocks sold at a cost of $4.00 each in prestige stores from coast to coast to the tune of 6,000 a day. An accompanying manual gave instructions on how to treat the rocks as human.

How strange that shapeless, inanimate objects should command human affection. But a Bible character, called a rock by Jesus, has been a favorite living stone of believers through the centuries.

When the teacher of an adult class was listing personality traits of the twelve disciples, a lady exclaimed, "I like Peter best of all!" Peter's impulsive blunderings and blusterings make him so human and so alive. Because we are so like him, we gravitate to his company.

But to think of Peter only as an impetuous, changeable braggart is to do him an injustice. We should never forget that this vacillating, oscillating fisherman became the solid, steady apostle who dominates the first half of Acts.

Those steadfast, sterling qualities that replaced the stumbling, bumbling indecision of his early years, and for the most part characterized his ministry from Pentecost on, should elicit our admiration and emulation.

The episodes used by the Master to transform Peter from clay into rock form the chapters of this book.

1

A New Name

(John 1:35–42)

Some years ago, while holding meetings out west, Dr. Haddon Robinson met a young pastor with little training but much potential.

Dr. Robinson, who for years headed up Dallas Seminary's pastoral theology department, spent time with this young pastor, urging him to secure more schooling.

The young pastor heeded Dr. Robinson's advice. God-given abilities, sharpened by formal training, ultimately led Dr. Earl Radmacher to the presidency of Western Baptist Seminary in Portland, Oregon. He readily admits that without the encouragement of Dr. Robinson he would not be where he is today.

Incidentally, in 1979 Dr. Robinson became president of Denver Baptist Seminary, Western's sister school. So, encourager and encouragee are now both presidents of Conservative Baptists' two seminaries.

The Lord Jesus met a young man whose temperament was unsteady, indecisive, and changeable. Seeing in Simon great potential, Jesus gave him a radically different name—"rock." That introduction to the Master triggered the beginning of a change in Simon's disposition from shifting sand to sturdy stone.

How did Simon come to meet the Master? What were the background factors in his conversion?

9

Home Influence

Simon (spelled Simeon in Acts 15:14) came originally from Bethsaida, but moved to Capernaum where he and his brother, Andrew, were partners with James and John in a fishing business (John 1:44; Matthew 8:5,14; Luke 5:10).

Probably around Jesus' age, Simon, who had never studied formally, was "unlearned" by the standards of his day (Acts 4:13). He was married, for he had a mother-in-law who lived with him in a home co-owned by Andrew. This joint ownership suggests that their father, Jona, may have died by this time (Mark 1:29,30; John 1:42).

Since Andrew and Simon were looking for the Messiah, these brothers likely came from a godly family, where their father had referred regularly to the Old Testament promises of a coming Messiah. Messianic expectation prevailed in those dark days. People were looking for an emancipator from the Roman yoke. For years reports had circulated of an angelic choir, a star, and a baby destined to be the deliverer. Some said that the 70 weeks of Daniel's vision were nearly finished. Probably Jona had spoken of these things to his sons. A godly home can provide strong influence toward conversion.

Public Preaching

Suddenly in those days, the populace was startled by a strange figure, a pale but wiry child of the desert, whose home was a cave, whose dress was camel's hair, whose food was wild locusts dipped in honey, and whose voice trumpeted, "Repent, for the kingdom is at hand!"

Peter, Andrew, and some friends joined the multitudes streaming down the Jordan valley to see John the Baptist. They heard him warn soldiers to do no violence, tax-collectors to be honest, and religious leaders to be genuinely repentant. Probably both Peter and Andrew answered his call, were baptized, and joined the ranks of those looking for the Messiah, of whom John was the forerunner.

Good home influence plus dynamic and sincere preaching have pointed many to the Messiah. But often a third element is involved.

Human Instrument

God usually uses a human instrument to augment family influence and pulpit ministry. The human instrument in winning Simon was his brother, Andrew, after his afternoon interview with the Lamb of God. Next day, basking in the inspiration of that long visit, and unable to keep it to himself, Andrew "first findeth his own brother Simon, and saith unto him, We have found the Messias, which is, being interpreted, the Christ. And he brought him to Jesus" (John 1:41–42a).

Though Andrew was to be overshadowed by Simon who would win the thousands, it was Andrew who won the one that won the thousands. Had not Andrew brought Simon, who would have preached at Pentecost? We never know how many we reach by bringing one. Only one lad won to Christ in a Scottish church in a whole year made the pastor wonder if his ministry was a failure. But that lad, Robert Moffatt, became a famous missionary whose daughter married David Livingstone. The one may be multiplied thousands of times over.

Moishe Rosen, founder of Jews for Jesus, and responsible, directly or indirectly, for winning hundreds of Jews to Christ, once told a congregation, "My wife isn't very good at soul-winning. In fact, she has won only three people to Christ—her two daughters and myself."

SIMON RECEIVED A NEW NAME—
ITS SIGNIFICANCE

Peter's conversion should not be confused with his call to service. Simon met the Savior when brought to Him by Andrew. Simon's call came months later when Jesus commanded him, along with Andrew, James, and John, to leave their nets and follow Him. This chapter deals with Simon's conversion. The next chapter will discuss his call.

At his conversion Simon was given a new name. At their very first meeting Jesus said, "Thou art Simon the son of Jona; thou shalt be called Cephas, which is by interpretation, A stone" (John 1:42).

Jewish custom bestowed new names on persons when a new epoch in their life was at hand, or a new characteristic was to be displayed. Abram, long before Sarah bore him a child, was given the new name of Abraham, which meant "father of many" (Genesis 17:5). Often on today's mission fields a convert is given a new name at his baptism to indicate he is dropping old ways to walk new paths.

Incongruity of Simon's New Name

Simon was anything but a stone. All four gospel writers agree in their delineation of him as impulsive, impetuous, and rash. Exasperating, though colorful, he blew hot and cold almost in the same breath. He dared to walk on water, but fearfully began to sink. He made a great confession which was a revelation from the Father, then rebuked Jesus with a remark that reeked with the breath of Satan. He told Jesus he would never let Him wash his feet, then moments later asked Jesus to wash him all over.

He affirmed he would die for Jesus, yet within hours declared three times with an oath that he never even knew Jesus. A blend of courage and cowardice, he sliced off the high priest's servant's ear in willing defense of Jesus, then not long later he slunk before a maid in denial of his Master. Yet Jesus called him "rock."

This new name would distinguish Simon from eight other Simons in the New Testament:

- the Cyrenian compelled to bear Jesus' cross (Luke 23:26);
- the Pharisee who invited Jesus for dinner (Luke 7:40);
- another of the Twelve (Matthew 10:4; Luke 6:15);
- a brother of Jesus (Matthew. 13:55);
- a healed leper (Matthew 26:6);
- father of Judas Iscariot (John 6:71);
- Sorcerer (Acts 8:9);
- and the tanner of Joppa (Acts 9:43).

Though this new name would distinguish Simon from all the others with the same name, Jesus gave it to him because He knew what Simon could and would become.

However, this new name must have sounded ridiculous to Andrew. "My brother a rock? How out of character! Doesn't Jesus know how unstable Simon is?" Perhaps Andrew had some temporary doubt about the Messiahship of Jesus. "Can Jesus really be the promised One when He calls Simon a rock?"

Jesus Knew What Simon Could Become

Jesus was not making any hasty, careless statement. When Andrew brought Simon, "Jesus beheld him" (John 1:42). "Beheld" meant that He studied him with a searching gaze. It was only after careful deliberation that Jesus called Simon a rock.

This new name indicated two things: first, that Jesus clearly understood where Simon's weakness lay; and second, what He would make of Simon by His grace. The Master would so exert influences in Simon's life that, despite his impulsive disposition and inconsistent deeds, he would come to hold the faith with persevering and contagious strength.

Michelangelo reportedly could visualize in slabs of marble, which others rejected, the forms which his creative genius would fashion into existence. Jesus saw in Simon the potentiality that His power would bring into actuality.

Encouragement to Peter

Though Andrew might have been puzzled at the new name given his brother, Simon must have been encouraged, as well as surprised. On his way to meet the Messiah, perhaps he said to himself, even out loud to Andrew, "I'm so hasty and unpredictable. How can I ever be of service to the Messiah?"

Then he heard his new name. New hope sprang within. "He certainly knows my weakness. How fickle I am. But to think He sees in me a rock!"

The new name awoke in Simon expectation of a great victory over his frailty. The Messiah would stabilize him. So Peter became a follower of Jesus, not only as Lamb of God to forgive his sins, but as stonecutter to refashion his life.

From the window of his second-floor studio in a downtown building an artist noticed a beggar who every day sat, asking alms by the busy corner. His clothes were tattered, his face dirty, his hair unkempt. With plaintive gaze and pleading voice he begged for coins. One morning the artist stood by the window to sketch the beggar, not as he looked, but as he might have looked had he worked at a job and kept up his appearance. Then opening the window, he beckoned the beggar to come up to the studio. The artist showed the beggar the painting. "Who is it?" the beggar asked. The artist replied, "You." "Me?" cried the beggar. "Yes," said the artist, "that is what I see in you." The beggar thought momentarily, then responded, "If that's the kind of man you see in me, that's the kind of man I'm going to be." He went out to secure a position and live respectably.

SIMON RECEIVED A NEW NAME—ITS REALIZATION

The Simon of the gospels seems so unlike the Peter of Acts. The changeable, cowardly Galilean became the courageous leader of the early church. He who had feared a maid faced thousands at Pentecost, unequivocally charging them with Jesus' death. Hauled before the Sanhedrin, the same court which so recently had condemned his Master, he undauntedly and repeatedly proclaimed Christ. Though beaten and forbidden to speak or teach in Jesus' name, he braved the wrath of the nation's religious leadership with a martyr-like spirit. Preaching and performing miracles, he was the mouthpiece of the apostolic band, and bulwark of strength to fellow-believers. Simon certainly lived up to his new name. He indeed became a rock.

Peter dominates the first twelve chapters of Acts before the story turns to trace the ministry of Paul. Though in the Gospels he is frequently called by his *Simon* name, in Acts he is referred to as *Peter* almost exclusively. (Simon is employed in the Cornelius episode where its use was necessary for the purpose of his identification by strangers.) Long before Acts was penned the new name had won out, the old transformed by the grace of God. Peter's rock-like character had emerged and had been recognized by his fellow-workers.

Interestingly, when Simon's close friend, John, wrote his Gospel over half a century later, he used the two names together, Simon Peter. This combination occurs frequently (1:40; 6:8,68; 13:6,9,24,36; 18:10,15,25; 20:2,6; 21:2, 3,7,11,15). Knowing him so well from the earliest day, John could never escape using his old *Simon* name, but noting the marvelous metamorphosis through the years, he called him also by his Christ-given title, Peter. Perhaps, too, a little bit of the old Simon cropped up now and again in the new Peter.

The New Name Involved a Process

Within sixty days of his denial of Jesus, Simon had made major strides toward strengthening his personality. But though he progressed toward stability, the old nature still lurked near the surface, biding its time to erupt in some wavering action.

Even a quarter century later Simon's early disposition asserted itself at Antioch. After eating with Gentile believers in a display of Christian liberty, he suddenly withdrew from their fellowship when Jewish believers with strong separatist views came on the scene from Jerusalem. He reasoned that his status with his Jewish brethren might be jeopardized by associating with Gentile believers. So momentary expediency prompted withdrawal from Gentile fellowship lest he offend his Jewish brethren (Galatians 2:12).

The Apostle Paul was God's instrument to confront Simon with his inconsistency. "Your withdrawal," Paul pointed out, "tacitly implies the necessity of keeping the Mosaic law in order to be saved, and is subtle denial of the gospel of grace" (vs. 14–20).

How hard it is to change! Our old habits cling tightly. But, as in previous reproofs, Peter probably acknowledged his error immediately and without reservation. Impetuous in his words and ways, he was just as hasty to mend his wrongs. Not a word indicates he acted otherwise. His ready acquiescence promoted both the unity of the body of Christ and his own personal spiritual growth.

For the rest of Peter's life the old and new natures

would do battle. Much of the time Peter would seem to be in control, then Simon would take over, as he blundered again. Peter was never able to quell the conflict until in heaven he saw his Master face-to-face, and in his glorified state was confirmed in holiness.

SIMON RECEIVED A NEW NAME— ITS IMPLICATIONS

Christ can see possibilities in us. He can speak of things that are not, as though they were. He saw in thunderous John the apostle of love. He discerned in crooked Zacchaeus an honest tax-collector. He beheld in the promiscuous woman of Samaria a faithful and virtuous witness. He perceived in fanatical persecuting Saul a zealous missionary of the despised cross.

An Old Testament parallel is the story of Gideon who was cowardly hiding in the hills, threshing wheat in the shadow of a big wine press. The unlikely hero was greeted by the angel of the Lord with these incongruous words, "The LORD is with thee, thou mighty man of valour" (Judges 6:12).

Just as He recognized in shaky Simon a solid rock, so as He gazes at us with all our frailties, debilities, vulnerabilities, and lapses, He can envision even in the quarry of our fallenness the strength of character into which He will fashion us.

We Need to See Possibilities in Others

Two speakers at a denominational convention in San Diego, California, gave credit on the same day to teachers who saw potential in them. Morning-lecturer Gordon MacDonald told how as a young man he came to Denver Baptist Seminary with a deficient outlook on things, but how a leader took him under his wing. He publicly thanked Dr. Vernon Grounds, present in that morning session, for having faith in him.

That evening the evangelist, Bill McKee, told how as a student at Northwestern Bible College in Minneapolis he was more interested in fun and dating than in studies and service. But men who saw his talents encouraged him, suggesting the opportunity of service overseas, involving a basketball team, which he accepted. Today he is a leading youth evangelist in the west. He thanked his mentors, who were present that night, for their patience with him.

Not only do we need to see and encourage possibilities in others, but we should also pray for them, as Christ prayed for Peter that his faith would not fail.

A Process for Us Too

When we meet Jesus as our Savior, we are born again. Just as physically a person does not remain an infant long, so the state of spiritual infancy does not have to last long. When Paul wrote the Corinthians his first letter, he expected the believers, though only a few years out of heathenism, to be sufficiently mature to be addressed as spiritual (3:1,2).

From this level of maturity the believer needs to grow. Peter listed qualities that should be added to our faith: virtue, knowledge, temperance, patience, godliness, kindness, and charity (2 Peter 1:5-7). True Christian experience is not a mere bubbliness of feeling, nor only mental assent to a system of doctrine, but it is character building as well. Truth is put into practice, or experience. This practice should become habitual. Habit settles into character which becomes permanent. Thus the stability of Christlikeness is created.

Temperament is a combination of inborn traits, strengths and weaknesses, that affect subconsciously a per-

son's behavior. We all fall into one of the following cat-
egories: sanguine, choleric, melancholic, or phlegmatic.
Though we form a mixture of all, one temperament will
predominate. But whatever our personality weakness, the
process of Christian growth can help us overcome the fault.
We take courage seeing how sanguine, warm, buoyant, impulsive, trigger-fingered, blustering Peter was purified, en-
nobled, and stabilized.

One lady said, "For years I would not look at people
directly. I was shy, withdrawn, and possessed little self-es-
teem. After I accepted Christ and grew in faith, Christ slowly
helped me to accept myself as a person of worth. Gradually
I was able to look at other people straight in the eye and
was no longer shy.

Are you hot-tempered? When you come to Christ, and
as He beholds you, He may call you, "Mr. Calm." Are
you a worrier? He may name you, "Mrs. Peace." Are you
covetous? He may address you, "Mr. Content." Are you
irritable, even ornery? He may name you, "Miss Sweet."
Are you homosexual or adulterous? He may term you, "Mr.
Pure."

We all come from a background of one common in-
gredient—imperfection. The church is composed of people
who are becoming more like Christ. One fellow wore a but-
ton, "Please be patient with me. GINFWMY." He explained
the initials as standing for, "God is not finished with me
yet."

The last recorded words of Peter command us to "grow
in grace, and in the knowledge of our Lord and Saviour
Jesus Christ" (2 Peter 3:18). He earlier told us how to grow.
"As newborn babes, desire the sincere milk of the word,
that ye may grow thereby" (1 Peter 2:2).

Twin dogs, both large and strong, would often fight.
When asked which one usually won, the owner replied,

"Whichever one I feed the most." Feeding milk and meat to our Peter-nature will help it gain the ascendency. Otherwise, the Simon-nature will get the victory.

As we progress in the process, winning more and more victories, we'll be able to say with John Newton,

> *"I am not what I ought to be,*
> *I am not what I want to be,*
> *I am not what I hope to be,*
> *But thank God,*
> *I am not what I used to be."*

Only when we see Jesus Christ face-to-face, shall we be perfectly like Him. In anticipation of the day of our glorification, we can say with the hymn writer,

> *"Then we shall be where we would be,*
> *Then we shall be what we should be,*
> *Things that are not now, nor could be,*
> *Soon shall be our own."*

The possibility of character change for Simon began when he was introduced to the Messiah. So for us, personality transformation requires first of all that we open our heart to the knock of Christ.

2

Call to Service

(Matthew 4:18–22; Mark 1:16–20;
Luke 5:1–11)

The fish, often displayed on bumper stickers or book covers, is a symbol of Christianity. The five letters of the Greek word for *fish* stand for: Jesus, Christ, God, Son, Savior. In the early days of persecution the fish was a secret sign between Christians. Many a fish was painted on the walls of the Catacombs.

The fish was connected with the Christian faith from the beginning. At least four of Jesus' disciples were fishermen. One of His parables likens the kingdom to a net which caught all kinds of fish. Both miraculous feedings of the 5,000 and the 4,000 involved fish. Jesus paid a tax by coin found in a fish's mouth. Twice the Lord gave his disciples huge catches of fish after fruitless nights of toil. On the first of these occasions He called Peter, along with three others, to follow Him fully.

Simon Peter had already come *to* Christ. Now he is commanded to come *after* Christ full time. His salvation was free, but his consecration would cost him everything.

Salvation precedes service, whether part or full time. One must first come *to* Christ before he can go *for* Christ. Sometimes Sunday school classes are taught, or youth groups led by, persons who have not yet met Jesus Christ as Savior. When a youth group from a liberal church came to an evangelistic rally in a gospel-preaching church, one of its advisors responded to the invitation to receive Christ. She commented, "I brought these young people to help them. Instead I got help. I was a leader, yet not a real believer."

PETER'S CALL WAS PRECEDED BY DEDICATED PART-TIME SERVICE

For months after his conversion Peter alternated between traveling with Jesus and fishing. Though he spent considerable time in the company of Jesus, he still devoted blocks of time to his employment as a fisherman.

Robertson's *Harmony of the Gospels* indicates that several well-known incidents in the life of Jesus took place when Peter was in Jesus' company but before Peter became a full-time follower. These include the miracle of turning water into wine at Cana, the chasing of the money changers out of the temple (John 2:12–17), the conversion of the notorious Samaritan woman, and the healing of the nobleman's son.

Though between tours Peter went back to his fishing, he is classified among Jesus' disciples at that time. It's not necessary to leave one's job to be a disciple. The Lord needs people to serve Him faithfully in all walks of life. Because it's impossible to separate the responsibilities of our secular life from our responsibilities to God, distinction between part-time and full-time service can become quite blurred. If God wills a person to remain at his desk or trade (where he usually has greater access to the unbelieving world), then is not that person really in the center of God's will, serving Him full-time?

But sometimes those who are doing what God wants them to do full-time in a secular occupation may be called by the Lord to surrender their occupation to devote all their time to His special service. May we then make a distinction between a full-time Christian and a Christian in full-time service? Peter, a full-time believer, though only part-time in the company of the Lord, now was asked to come full-time with the Lord. He was called to leave his fishing business and yield wholly to the job of fishing for men.

Testing and Training Period

Before calling Peter to come full-time with Him Jesus gave him a foretaste of the work, not only an inkling of His healing ministry, but a lesson in what would be Peter's major—fishing for men.

Peter observed first-hand Jesus' dealing with the Samaritan woman, an unlikely candidate for acceptance because she was a woman, a half-breed Samaritan, and immoral, having lived with six men though she had never married. Then, along with other disciples, he was sent on a reaping expedition in fields white unto harvest. The winning of these many Samaritans foreshadowed the massive "fishing" assignment planned for Peter and the apostles in the yet-to-be-given Great Commission.

Even in this early period Jesus let Peter and other part-time disciples baptize new converts (John 4:1–2). Enjoyment and success on this part-time basis encouraged Peter to respond affirmatively when the full-time call came.

The Lord doesn't usually make full-time lights out of people who fail to shine during part-time opportunities. The seminary student who refuses to teach Sunday school class because he feels called to preach to hundreds may never get an invitation to a pastorate. A young man told a missionary home on furlough from Africa, "Some day I hope to do missionary work in your country." "What mission work are you doing here now?" "Oh, none," he replied.

Advised the missionary, "Then, please don't come to Africa to do it."

Before any church will call a pastor, or any mission board accept a candidate, examiners want evidence that the prospect has had some ability, delight, and even success in his current Christian ministry, even if in a limited measure. Those early days of discipleship gave Peter such assurance.

Also, this pre-call period gave Peter time to learn more of the Master. Was this peasant-carpenter really the Messiah? Peter observed the miracles, heard His matchless words, and above all, saw His incomparable example.

PETER'S CALL WAS TAILORED TO HIS PARTICULAR SITUATION

The Lord usually calls His servants when they are at work. Moses was minding his flock when God spoke in the burning bush. David, likewise, was watching sheep when called to greater tasks. Matthew was working at his tax-collecting booth. Peter was fishing when Christ beckoned.

A Call by the Sea

It was early morning on the Lake of Galilee, called the most sacred sheet of water on earth, roughly seven by thirteen miles, 700 feet below sea level. Its shores were dotted with prosperous towns and villages, now awakening to the hum of activity as the waters rippled under the early morning breeze. Fishing was its main industry.

For Jesus, who moved from Nazareth to Capernaum during the early period of His ministry (Matthew 4:13), His sphere of labor had been a carpenter shop. But for Peter, his bailiwick was the sea of Galilee.

Fruitless Night

Along with other fishermen, Peter and Andrew had been out all night but had caught nothing. Suddenly, around a bend in the shore came a crowd, following Jesus, wanting to hear His every word of wisdom. Though all three Gospels tell the story, Luke's account is fullest, amplifying the sketchiness of Matthew and Mark.

As the crowd pressure built up, Jesus spotted two empty boats from which Peter and his partners had stepped to tend their nets. Boarding Peter's boat, Jesus asked him to thrust out a little from land, so He could more conveniently teach the constantly growing multitude. When He finished teaching, Jesus asked him to launch out into the deep and to let down his nets for a catch.

Typically, Peter's reaction wavered between doubt and faith, "Master, we have toiled all the night, and have taken nothing" (Luke 5:5). As if to say, "We're experienced fishermen. You're an outsider, what do you know about the sea and fishing? I assure you it's no use. If we haven't caught anything during the night, how likely are we to catch anything now in the daylight? We just finished washing our nets. And you want me to soil them again, and without reasons." Then Peter added, "Nevertheless at thy word I will let down the net" (vs. 5).

Unexpected Success

When Peter and Andrew let down the net, so many fish were enclosed that the net broke. Muscles bulged, as they struggled with the net. Perspiration broke out on their foreheads. They had to summon their partners, James and John, for help. As they piled the silver cargo into both boats, the load was so heavy they began to sink.

The miracle dazzled Peter. "He fell down at Jesus' knees, saying, Depart from me; for I am a sinful man, O Lord" (vs. 8). Though Peter had known Jesus for some months, suddenly the supernatural glory of His essential nature dawned on Peter's heart. He saw his own sinfulness as he felt the tug of the breaking net and the sinking of the overloaded boat.

A person who is aware of his sinfulness and of treatment better than he deserves, will be ready for the service of soul-winning. Overwhelmed by inadequacy and grace, Peter was ripe for Jesus' call, "Simon, Fear not; from henceforth thou shalt catch men" (vs. 10). Matthew and Mark phrase it, "Come ye after me, and I will make you (to become) fishers of men."

Immediate Response

Obedience was immediate. Peter left nets, boats, business, father, and all, and followed Jesus. F. B. Meyer imagines the conversation between Peter and his wife, as he stops home to explain, "Can you spare me for a while? The Master has called me to follow Him. He will provide for you. He wants me in some great work."

She replies, "Mother and I can get along. We were just saying this morning that you've become a different man since you met the Master." In later years Peter was to take his wife along on apostolic journeys (1 Corinthians 9:5).

Peter left behind a comfortable existence to follow a Master who had no apparent income, except some support from faithful women of means (Luke 8:1–3). Neither did the Master have a place to lay His head. Peter would not return home every few days, but would be with Jesus constantly, sleeping on hillsides and in fields if necessary. Peter responded to a call asking for toil, travel, hardship, and renunciation.

Appeal on Level of Experience

The Master-Teacher always proceeded from the known to the unknown. Peter knew all about fishing for fish; now he would learn about fishing for men. Many of the strategies he would discover to be similar. For example, a fisherman tries to keep out of sight, no splashing around. The soul-winner must be tactful and winsome.

The fisherman needs to know the best bait. Soul-winners must know human nature and how to approach people.

Fishermen require patience and persistence, sometimes waiting a long time for a bite. Fishers of men "must not strive; but be gentle unto all men, apt to teach, patient, in meekness instructing those that oppose themselves; if God peradventure will give them repentance to the acknowledging of the truth" (2 Timothy 2:24).

Fishermen must know the habits of fish, when and where they are biting, and go where they are. Peter would watch Jesus in the company of publicans and sinners and observe how He won the lost. An English coastal preacher told how one morning a number of boats came to an inlet near his home, a place no boats had ever come before. The crews had discovered a shoal of fish and were cautiously pursuing them. Then the preacher commented, "The church must go where men congregate to win them. If they will not come to our churches, let's go out of our churches after them. Let's organize visitation from home to home. We must follow sinners to their house, aye, even to their ale-houses."

The late Sam Shoemaker, Episcopalian bishop, warned, "In the Great Commission the Lord has called us to be like Peter—fishers of men. We've turned the commission around so that we have become merely keepers of the aquarium. Occasionally, I take some fish out of your fishbowl and put them into mine, and you do the same with my bowl. But we're all tending the same fish."

A major difference exists between fishing for fish and fishing for people. In the former, the fisherman catches that which is alive, but then dies. In the latter, the soul-winner catches that which is dead in sin, but then comes to have eternal life. An older book on soul-winning bore this title, *Taking Men Alive.*

The Master's call appealed to the adventurous in Peter. Still today, no greater thrill exists than having a share in someone's finding new life in Christ.

PETER'S CALL WAS FOLLOWED BY NEEDED LESSONS

Peter had to learn many lessons before he could become the rock-like fisher of men. A few days after his call, likely the next Sabbath, a whirlwind succession of events must have left an indelible impression on him. In the morning Jesus spoke in the synagogue but was interrupted by a demon-possessed man. He healed him. Entering Peter's house, Jesus cured his mother-in-law of a fever, who then rose to minister to all of them. In the evening "all the city" brought to Peter's door a crowd of their sick. Jesus healed them. Early next morning Jesus went out to a lonely place, soon followed by Peter and his friends (Mark 1:21–38).

This vivid passage has been termed "the memory of the greatest day in Peter's life." It has also been called "the day when his discipleship had begun" (*The Life and Teaching of Jesus Christ by Arthur Headlam*, p. 11).

F. B. Mayer suggests four lessons Peter needed to prepare him for his life's work, and which were all exhibited on this memorable Sabbath day so soon after his call.

1. *Fishing for men would involve a struggle against the powers of spiritual darkness* (Mark 1:21–28)

It must have been an awkward moment when the shrill

voice of a demon-possessed man broke the silence of the worship in the synagogue that Sabbath morn. His cry was, "Let us alone; what have we to do with thee, thou Jesus of Nazareth?" But the Lord was unruffled by the disturbance. He rebuked the unclean spirit, ordering it to leave its victim.

This miracle made Peter recognize the existence of a vast underworld of spirits capable of unleashing violent opposition against anyone who tried to rescue victims from their Satanic influence.

Fishing for men would require the power of Christ for defeat of the enemy.

2. *Fishing for men would require compassion and gentleness* (Mark 1:29–31)

By nature, Peter was blustery and heavy-footed. His step would crush a bruised reed and quench smoking flax.

But observing Jesus gently deal with his fever-ridden mother-in-law, as He tenderly took her by the hand and lifted her up, was something he could never forget.

Little did he know that before many years he would be touching fevered brows, lifting the lame, even restoring the dead. By then tenderness would temper toughness. In later life he would write, "Having compassion one of another, love as brethren, be pitiful, be courteous" (1 Peter 3:8).

3. *Fishing for men would need a glimpse into the anguish of the world* (Mark 1:32–34)

At sunset a piteous gathering of those who were ill were carried to Peter's house and parked at his door. What a crowd! What a variety of illnesses! And what burdens of agonized friends!

If every house should expose its hurts and woes, or if one could hear the groans of those hospitalized, or shut-in, or mentally ill, or deeply burdened, what a vast array of misery and pain, what a host of needy and miserable. The servant of Christ must be sensitive to the broken-hearted, the spiritually wounded, and especially to those who are lost and do not know Him.

4. *Fishing for men requires knowledge of the source of power* (Mark 1:35–39)

Very early next morning Jesus slipped away to a lonely place to pray. When Peter went to awaken Jesus (perhaps another crowd was gathering at the door), Jesus was gone. Peter and his friends had an idea where he would be. Starting out to search, they may have met a fisherman returning from his night's toil who said, "I saw Him climbing that hill." Finally they found him in a lonely spot, kneeling in prayer. They said, "All men seek for thee."

He replied, "Let us go into the next towns, that I may preach there also: for therefore came I forth."

Jesus wanted to fish for men in other towns, but He knew that strength for the day's activities would come only by prayer. He couldn't do what He did apart from seeking God's face.

Peter learned this lesson well. Before Pentecost he was found with the 120 in the upper room praying. Prayer dominated the atmosphere of the early church of which Peter was the central figure (Acts 2:42; 3:1; 4:23–31).

The Greatest Catch

Peter's greatest fishing expedition took place at Pentecost, when he landed 3,000 souls. He went on to win countless more.

Down through the centuries Christ has called His fishermen, whose all-consuming passion has been to take men alive for the Master. Robert Moffat, father-in-law of David

Livingstone, asked to write in a lady's album, penned the following lines:

> *"My album is in savage breasts,*
> *Where passion reigns and darkness rests,*
> *Without one ray of light;*
> *To write the name of Jesus there,*
> *To point to world both bright and fair,*
> *And see the pagan bow in prayer,*
> *Is all my soul's delight."*

In the mid-'40s a drunken derelict stumbled into the doorway of New York City's Jerry McAuley Cremorne Mission on 42nd Street, to get out of the rain. A few days later he accepted Christ and was delivered of his drinking habit. Two years later, on the anniversary of his conversion, he was made superintendent of the mission. Seven years later, on January 14, 1955, he died after a long illness. At his crowded funeral service it was estimated that in those few years, because of his familiarity with the haunts and habits of the derelicts in the neighborhood, he had been able to win over 9,000 men to Christ. He was indeed a modern fisher of men.

God wants us devoted to Him fully, whether or not we are in full-time service. The Lord Jesus was following His Father's will completely when working as a carpenter the first thirty years of his life. But the day came when to follow His Father's will meant leaving the carpenter's shop and launching out full-time on His public ministry.

Matthew probably kept his job as a tax-collector even after he became a disciple of Jesus, alternating between periods at his toll-booth and tours in ministry with Jesus. But when the Master bade him follow fully, Matthew rose, left behind his books, debits, credits, and toll-house, and joined Jesus' group full-time.

In a youth crusade in a Canadian church back in 1936, approximately 100 young people presented themselves for all-out consecration to the Lord. For many, this meant remaining in their secular jobs as full-time disciples. But for dozens of others, it resulted in a call to discipleship in full-time service. Today these people are serving as pastors, missionary doctors, missionary executives, missionary educators, missionary pilots, and so on.

Were we to ask these folks, or Matthew, or Peter, "Why did you forsake business, boats and all to follow Jesus? all would answer the same way,

> *"I heard His call, 'Come follow,'*
> *That was all.*
> *My gold grew dim,*
> *My soul went after Him,*
> *I rose and followed.*
> *That was all.*
> *Who would not follow*
> *If they heard Him call?"*

33

Walking on Water

(Matthew 14:22–33)

Tornadoes ripped through the northern Indiana college town of Goshen in the spring of 1955, killing 27 persons and destroying 134 houses in less than a square mile area. A Goshen College sociological study reported a year later that people who lived through those storms displayed more anxiety as a result. Survivors often worried over family members late getting home. On the other hand, the report indicated that 81 percent showed more awareness of others' needs, tried to help, confided more in their spouses, interacted more with neighbors, and relied more on human relationships.

A psychological study of the effect of storms on the disciples would have been interesting, for they were subject to periodic, sudden, violent squalls on the sea of Galilee. Without warning, tempests would funnel down through encircling hills on to this below-sea-level lake, churning its waters into a boiling cauldron, with billows as high as six feet.

During one such turbulence Jesus came walking on the waves toward the disciples' tossing boat. Impetuous Peter asked if he could walk on the water too.

PETER'S PREDICAMENT—IN A STORM NOT OF HIS MAKING

Some storms that strike our life may be of our own making. By running away from God Jonah caused the tempest that struck his boat. The stubbornness of the centurion who disregarded Paul's warning to follow the advice of the ship's captain landed the passengers in the midst of a storm that hid the sun for two weeks and tossed them helplessly on the Mediterranean.

Some storms are of Satanic origin, like the "great wind from the wilderness" which smote the house where Job's seven sons and three daughters were dining, killing them all.

But the disciples found themselves in a storm because of the explicit order of their Master. Right after Jesus miraculously fed the 5,000, the multitude wanted to make Him king by force. Knowing His popularity stemmed from His ability to provide food, He sought solitude. But first He insisted "his disciples . . . get into a ship, and . . . go before Him unto the other side, while he sent the multitudes away. And when he had sent the multitudes away, he went up into a mountain apart to pray: and when the evening was come, he was there alone" (Matthew 14:22,23).

Jesus had to virtually force them into the boat, perhaps because they wanted to be with Him if the crowd was going to make Him king. Or likely they sensed a storm. With a squall brewing it was no night for crossing the sea.

But Jesus knew that struggling in a storm would be less dangerous than staying with the wrong crowd. Sometimes a storm is the place of greatest moral security, for its demands on our attention and energies keep us from yielding to a temptation which is becoming too much for us. Out on the storm-tossed waves the disciples had no time to ponder making Jesus a superficial king.

The Christian life is not a pleasant little canoe trip down some gently-flowing stream. Nor is it a perpetual picnic with the sun always shining bright and golden. Storms do upset the calm of believers' lives, often suddenly, unexpectedly, in areas of health, family, job, or finances, bringing disappointment, discouragement, depression, defeat, loneliness, rejection, frustration, helplessness, or fear.

As the disciples headed for the other side, they encountered a squall. They struggled hard against wind and wave. They became distressed. Simon and the others wondered if the Lord was aware of their predicament.

PETER'S HELPER—NOT FORGOTTEN BY THE LORD

Though the disciples didn't know where Jesus was, Jesus knew where they were. His eye was fixed on that tossing little craft. Even when He prayed on the mountain, they were in His thoughts, and in the hollow of His hand.

On an earlier occasion when the disciples had been caught in a violent storm on Galilee, Jesus had been in the boat with them, though asleep. Awakened by their plea, "Carest thou not that we perish?", Jesus had subdued the elements. But this time they were in the storm alone, so they thought. However, they were to learn an advanced lesson—that though He was miles away physically, He was present spiritually, watching over them.

The Christian who finds himself in the midst of tempestuous trials can rest in the assurance that the Lord is never out of the picture, but is watching over and praying for him. When Philip Armour, meat-packing magnate, was a young man, a banker called, "I'm worried about your

loan at our bank." Armour replied, "No use both of us
worrying over the same thing," and hung up.

A bishop had trouble sleeping one night as he worried
over the spiritual state of the fifty churches under his ju-
risdiction. When the clock hit midnight, he seemed to hear
a voice, "Now go to bed, Bishop, I'll sit up the rest of
the night."

As long as a trial is raging, the eye of the Lord is
upon us. Peter learned his lesson well. Years later, in prison
and scheduled for execution the next morning, he was able
to sleep so soundly that an angel had to hit him on the
side in order to awaken him.

Jesus Did Not Come Immediately

Jesus didn't come to them the minute they found themselves in the storm. When Mary and Martha sent for Jesus
because of Lazarus's serious illness, Jesus waited two days
still in the place where He was, giving Lazarus time to die.
He could have come at once but didn't. The sisters exclaimed
on His arrival, "If thou hadst been here, my brother had
not died." Jesus wanted to perform the greater miracle of
resurrection.

Jesus long delayed coming to the disciples. Suppose
as late as 9 P.M. He ordered the disciples into the boat.
It wasn't till the fourth watch that He came, or between
3 and 6 A.M. The headwind was so strong that they rowed
a minimum of six hours to cover 25 to 30 furlongs (roughly
three miles), a maximum speed of one-half mile an hour
(Matthew 14:25; John 6:19).

Jesus came in the darkest hour of the night, just before
dawn. So Jesus comes to us in our storms today, not when
the storm starts, not when we send for Him, but after much
delay and often at the darkest hour.

Jesus Came in an Unexpected Way

Who would have expected Him to come using the water as pavement for His approach. He used the very waves that threatened to swallow them, showing His mastery over the frightful elements. Cowper put it,

> *"God moves in a mysterious way*
> *His wonders to perform,*
> *He plants His footsteps on the sea*
> *And rides upon the storm. "*

The disciples may have figured out how they wanted their Master to rescue them, but He came His own way. Through the darkness, foam and mist, they caught a glimpse of a form moving majestically toward them, walking on the frothy, mountainous waves. What a sight!

In the midst of their confusion, yelling at each other what to do and how to row, they all saw Him and were frightened. They wanted deliverance but not by this new way of doing things. Thinking it was a spirit, they cried out in fear.

A boy, afraid of the dark, wouldn't go out at night, lest something "get me." His mother tried to reassure him, "Go out and play, son. You'll be all right. God is out there and He'll take care of you." Peering into the dark, and taking one careful step outside, he spoke boldly, "Okay, God, if you're out there, don't move a muscle, or you'll scare me to death."

Jesus Dispelled Their Fear

Identifying Himself, Jesus said, "Be of good cheer; it is I: be not afraid." What an unnatural announcement if He were only man. What a natural announcement if He were truly God.

The ancient Egyptian symbol of impossibility was the simple figure of two feet planted on a fragment of ocean. By making a liquid pavement He proved Himself ruler of all nature. Before taking them out of the storm, He took the storm out of them.

If we would have calm in storm, our faith must be linked to the Person of our blessed Lord. We must see Him in the fullness of His Godhead, commanding and controlling the elements. We must recognize Him as Master of the universe, the Lord of the elements.

PETER'S RESPONSE: HIS LITTLE FAITH

As soon as Jesus identified Himself Peter, overwhelmed by this demonstration of divine power, called out, "Lord, if it be thou, bid me come unto thee on the water." How wonderful that we can talk to the Lord in the storms of life!

Why such a request? Was Peter trying to pull some stunt, "See how great I am. I can walk on water!" Not likely. Rather it was typically Peter, impulsive and impetuous, anxious to get closer to Christ faster than by staying in the boat.

Jesus didn't reply, "Foolish man. You ask the impossible." There was no put-down, but simply "Come." Jesus indulged Peter's whim, using it to develop firmer faith, for he was still far from being the rock that Jesus intended.

Peter started out magnificently. Climbing out of the boat, he walked on the water toward Jesus. Up to the top of a wave with all its foam he went, then down the other side into the hollow, then back up the next wave.

Then something happened. He began to panic. Was it because he had gotten a noseful of water. Not likely, for he had been soaked many times in Galilean squalls. As he began to notice the strength of the wind as it howled boisterously, his eyes wandered from Jesus to the waves, so that he began to sink.

Tino Wallenda of the famous high-wire performing family says, "When I walk the wire I must concentrate definitely on the other side. I keep my eyes straight ahead. If I start to look over to the audience or watch somebody underneath me, there is a good possibility I could lose my balance. It's the same thing with Jesus. You have to keep your eyes straight ahead and straight on Jesus. Otherwise you are going to fall to one side or the other. You may regain your balance and come back in line with God, if you do get into trouble, but why not keep your eyes on Jesus and stay out of trouble" (Christian Life, July 1979).

Peter should not have been distracted by the waves. Dr. Martin Lloyd-Jones suggests that Peter had not really dealt with the problem of the waves before leaving the boat. The old Peter mentality had displayed itself again. Reverting to his impulsiveness, Peter had acted without thinking it through. He should have reasoned, "The waves are wild and high. But the Master is walking on them. With His help I can walk on them, too." But he failed to handle the question of the waves before stepping out into their full furry. So he wavered.

How easy for today's child of God to get his eyes off the Lord and on to problems. We may imagine all sorts of illness. The pile of bills may seem mountainous. Disappointment, heartache, and tragedy may seem to stalk us. But does God ever break His Word? Is any situation beyond His power? Have His promises been abolished? Has He been pushed off His throne?

Peter was learning a needed lesson in the process of growing in stability. Thinking he was stronger than he was, he received a reminder of his weakness, and of the necessity of leaning more fully on the Rock of Ages. Someone put it, "The tougher the going, the faster the growing." This experience should have warned him against later overconfidence when he boasted he would never deny Christ.

Beginning to sink, Peter cried, not for a rope from Andrew but for help from Christ. It was a short prayer—just three words, "Lord, save me." Had Peter prayed like the average Sunday morning preacher, he would have been at the bottom of Galilee before he finished. Most Bible prayers are short. Perhaps we need shorter public petitions and longer private prayers.

Immediately Jesus stretched forth His hand, grabbing Peter and saying, "O thou of little faith, wherefore didst thou doubt?" Peter was lifted by the hand that tossed the stars into space, scooped out the ocean beds, carved the mountains and painted the sunsets. Someone said, "Before Jesus rebuked the doubter, He saved the sinker." Even when our faith is weak, no one is able to pluck us out of His hand, nor separate us from His love.

Peter walked with Jesus back to the ship. Suddenly the wind ceased. The disciples worshiped Him, saying, "Of a truth thou art the Son of God."

A church in Oregon was severely damaged by a flash flood. In one Sunday school room hung a picture of the Lord Jesus walking on water. Unbelievably the water mark on the wall indicated the flood had stopped just beneath Jesus' feet. God is able to control the height to which the waters of adversity reach in our lives.

PETER'S FAITH—HIS ADVENTURESOME SPIRIT

What possessed Simon to step out on such a tempestuous sea? Let's congratulate him for his adventuresome spirit, even though his faith may have wavered. The Lord didn't charge him with no faith. His rebuke for little faith was indirectly an acknowledgement of some faith. No other disciple showed any trust then. Only Peter took steps of faith to walk a bridge over troubled waters.

Peter actually walked on water. If he walked only a yard before he sank, what a thrill he must have had. In addition, he walked back with Jesus to the boat. Whether Jesus had to hold Peter up on the return walk, just hold his hand, or let him walk alone, how wonderful for Peter to experience the sensation of buoyancy over tossing waves.

The key is faith, whether small or great. Only twice did Jesus commend great faith, once to a Roman centurion, and then to a Canaanite mother, both of whom begged healing for their children.

Ever wonder what the other disciples thought of Peter's escapade? Wouldn't every last one of them wish he had done what Peter did, even with his sinking faith. Better to be believing Peter wet than doubting Thomas dry. Only Peter of all the Twelve could say, and with humility, "I walked on water." This episode would help Peter to face later storms. As he went from council to council, from prison to prison, from trial to trial, he would also go from faith to faith.

Peter was never rebuked for trying. Those who remain in the boat never sink. But if we want to walk on water, we have to climb out of the boat.

An adventuresome spirit is needed in the secular world. The man who headed the U.S. Patent Office in the 1880s wanted to shut down the office because everything had been invented. During the past 15 years alone, one million patents have been granted, and three times as many Ph.D. scientists are at work as have worked in the entire previous history of science.

Abraham ventured for God. Answering God's call, he went out, not knowing where he was going. Hebrews 11 portrays a gallery of heroes who walked on water by faith.

The late Dr. V. R. Edman imagined the questions thrown at the three wise men by their friends on hearing of their proposed trip westward.

"You're going to search for a king, and you don't know his name?"

"Palestine is so far away. How can they have a king when they're under Rome?"

"You say this new king is a Jew. But they have no royal family, nor kingdom of their own."

"You don't know how long you'll be gone. Nor how much the journey will cost you. Nor where this king is. Yet you call yourselves wise men. Seems like a foolish venture for wise men to undertake."

"You talk about a star in the sky. Why, the sky is full of stars every clear night. How can you tell which star is for your Jewish king? You wise men aren't as wise as you think."

But the Magi walked on water and found the Messiah.

Despite the opposition of ministers who declared that if God willed to convert the heathen He would do it without the aid of men, William Carey believed the Great Commission demanded missionaries taking the Gospel to all the nations of the world. Notwithstanding his poverty, Carey managed to master Latin, Greek, and Hebrew, while acquiring a wide knowledge of natural history and botany, all of this while working at his cobbler's bench. In 1793 he and his family sailed for India. Against almost insuperable obstacles he translated the Bible, in whole or in part, into 24 Indian languages, making the Word of God accessible to more than 300,000,000 people. He also prepared grammars and dictionaries of several tongues, as well as writing articles on the natural history and botany of India. He exemplified his motto, "Attempt great things for God; expect great things from God."

George Muller stepped out on trust to care for 10,000

orphans over a period of half a century. Never did the orphans go without a meal, though as many as 2,000 were living at the orphanage at one time. Though he made it a policy never to make known his needs, over five million dollars came in by "walking on water" faith.

Peter acted on impulse in asking to come over water to Jesus. Though we would not recommend irrational behavior as normal procedure, at times we must act on impulse if we are to obey the Spirit. One Sunday morning a derelict staggered into a fashionable church and slumped on the rear seat. When every few moments he mumbled in hoarse tones, some of the congregation stared ahead, while others chuckled mildly. Finally, an elder, acting on impulse, walked back, sat beside the derelict, put his arm around him, and soothed him the rest of the service. Afterward the impulsive man learned that the street man was homeless, and had suffered marital, financial, and physical tragedies. Assistance given the man helped lead him to a later decision to follow Christ. The elder who acted on impulse never regretted his unplanned action. Perhaps others in nearby pews sat indifferent, perhaps even resisting the impulse to help. One mark of Christian maturity is the ability to recognize the gentle leading of the Spirit and then act quickly on that leading.

Thin is the line between faith and presumption. A new convert in the excitement of his fresh faith decided on his own to rent a football stadium for a youth rally. Questions like, "Where will we get the money?" and "Where will we get the crowd?" never entered his mind. The affair was a disaster both financially and attendance-wise. Perhaps Paul's qualification for a church leader as "not a novice" was partly a protection against impulsively presumptive, out-of-the-will-of-God decisions by church officials.

One day three young men came to see the late President V. Raymond Edman in his office at Wheaton College.

Dressed in work-clothes, for they were earning their way through school, they related their vision of a Christian radio station in Liberia, Africa. Later Dr. Edman admitted he thought their plan a foolish, impossible dream, but because God might have put this stir in their hearts, he prayed with them for the thousands of dollars needed. Years later Dr. Edman said, "I visited ELWA, a powerful, influential station operated by the Sudan Interior Mission in Liberia, Africa," which had come into existence through the faith of these young men.

We hear much about the need for goal-setting. We are told goals should be specific, reachable, and accountable. Perhaps, however, we would now and again select goals a little beyond our grasp, those difficult or seemingly unreachable.

Yet, with the help of God we can laugh at impossibilities and cry, "It shall be done."

Peter and the Keys

(Matthew 16:13–25; Mark 8:27–33;
Luke 9:18–23)

A seminary professor imagines modern theologians, Barth, Brunner, and Tillich, meeting the Lord Jesus who asks them, "Whom do men say that I am?" Then after their answer, the Lord asks, "But whom do you say that I am?"

Barth, Brunner, and Tillich gave this learned answer, "Thou art the ground of being; thou art the leap of faith into the impenetrable unknown; thou art the existential, unphraseable, unpropositional confrontation with the infinity of inherent, subjective, experience."

To the same question Simon Peter gave a much simpler, more direct, and more accurate answer.

Peter, a dominant personality, was indisputably leader among the twelve disciples. In every listing of the disciples his name comes first (Matthew 10:2; Mark 3:16; Luke 6:14; John 21:2; Acts 1:13). Among the inner three he is named first (Matthew 17:1; Mark 5:37). In fact, in one list he is specifically called "first" (Matthew 10:2).

Peter was spokesman for the Twelve. Sometimes when a gospel reports a statement directed by the disciples to Jesus, another Gospel singles out Peter, in particular, as the speaker (Matthew 15:15 and Mark 10:28; Matthew 18:21 and Mark. 11:21).

On occasion Peter is the only one in a group of disciples

mentioned by name. It's Simon or Peter "and they that were with him" (Mark 1:36; Luke 8:45; 9:32).

Outsiders regarded Peter as ringleader. It was he whom the Capernaum tax-collectors approached about his Master's tax payment (Matthew 17:24). With his outgoing spontaneity, Peter stood out as leader.

The Roman Catholic church goes far beyond the leadership concept. It holds the absolute authority of Peter, not only over the other apostles but over the church universal, making him supreme Primate, Monarch, and Pastor of all Christian people of all centuries. Their claim is based on their interpretation of Peter as the rock on which Christ promised to build His church, and to whom He gave the keys of the kingdom (Matthew 16: 16–18).

The above passage begins with Jesus asking a searching question, to which Peter gave a magnificent confession. Then it was that Jesus bestowed a high honor on Peter. But immediately after came a stern rebuke to the apostles, followed by a solemn demand on all would-be disciples.

A SEARCHING QUESTION

For over two years Jesus had lived among His disciples, making Himself of no reputation. Though He had been pointed out as the Lamb of God by John the Baptist, though He had performed miracles, though His words made indelible impact, up to now He had not declared Himself the Christ.

With about a year left before He would leave them, they needed to crystallize their conviction as to who He was. If they were to be His witnesses to the ends of the earth, they would need to know the identity of the One of whom they witnessed. Now was the time for Jesus to draw them out to full recognition of His person.

So, while the band of disciples was traveling near Caesarea Philippi, a beautiful spot 40 miles above Capernaum, just a few miles from Dan, northern extremity of the Holy Land, Jesus asked, "Whom do men say that I the Son of man am?" (Matthew 16:13).

That Jesus was no ordinary man was widely recognized. The air was thick with opinions as to who He was. Many a person had his particular view, ready to enlighten his hearers at a moment's notice. In answer to Jesus' question the disciples mentioned the current theories: John the Baptist back from the dead; Elijah, great prophet whom Malachi predicted; or Jeremiah, weeping prophet; or one of the old prophets risen. But none said "the Christ."

All these answers came from the court of public opinion. So Jesus turned to the court of private opinion, by asking a personal question, "But whom say ye that I am?" Though concerned with what others thought, He was much more interested in the response of His disciples.

A MAGNIFICENT CONFESSION

As Jesus waited for the answer to His question, He knew the disciples would never side with the Pharisees in calling Him a dangerous sorcerer in league with the prince of demons. Nor would they join those who accused Jesus of being "beside Himself." Surely they would consider Him far more than "the carpenter's son." And hopefully more than a risen John the Baptist, a second Elijah, or another Jeremiah.

The answer was not long in coming. Without hesitation, emphatically, decisively, unequivocally, from the lips of Peter came the majestic confession, "Thou art the Christ, the Son of the living God." Once again it was Peter who led the way with an answer that did not disappoint his Master.

Peter seems to have made a similar confession on an earlier occasion when many professing disciples went back to walk no more with Jesus. When Jesus asked the Twelve, "Will ye also go away?", Peter answered, "Lord, to whom shall we go? thou hast the words of eternal life. And we believe and are sure that thou art that Christ, the Son of the living God" (John 6:68,69). However, earlier manuscripts have Peter calling Jesus, not "that Christ," but "the Holy One of God," a recognition which according to the Pulpit Commentary, though true, falls short of his confession in Caesarea Philippi.

Source of Peter's Confession

How did Peter arrive at this conclusion? Had he been impressed by the miracles, discourses, and character of Jesus? A formidable apologetic for the deity of Christ can be built from His works, words, and worth. Whoever performed, spoke, or lived like Him? Yet more was needed.

This confession wasn't a wild leap of faith in the dark, made up on the spur of the moment, nor was he parroting a second-hand viewpoint. The source of Peter's affirmation was heavenly. Said Jesus, "Flesh and blood hath not revealed it unto thee, but my Father which is in heaven."

What led Peter to utter this confession is what always leads men to reach the same belief today. No one is led to faith solely through preaching, apologetics, or the example of others, though these may play a vital part in directing a person toward Christ. R. V. S. Tasker, New Testament Professor at King's College, University of London, says, "Unless the Spirit of the living God is at work in the human heart, the deductions of reason, however convincing, will not lead to a life of active discipleship; the example of others, however inspiring, will have but a temporary influence; and the message of the Gospel, however faithfully proclaimed, will fall on soil where it takes no permanent root. Only the Holy Spirit can take of the things of Jesus and so reveal them to us that we are led to make with Peter the great confession, 'You are the Christ, the Son of the living God' (*Christianity Today,* 18 February 1957, *Peter's Confession,* p. 7-8).

"What think ye of Christ" is still the most pointed, searching question that can be asked a person today. Because of Christ's massive impact on the world's music, art, and literature, and because of His powerful gift of enlightenment, freedom, and purpose to mankind through the centuries, indifference to the issue of His person, work, and claims, borders on intellectual dishonesty.

The answer to this question determines present life-style, and more importantly, one's eternal destiny. Everything in the here and hereafter depends on what we think of Jesus, God's Son. To insult the Son is to slap God in the face. It's impossible to actively hate or passively neglect the Lord Jesus without displeasing His Father. The Apostle John wrote, "He that honoureth not the Son honoureth not the Father which hath sent him" (5:23). Paul wrote, "If any man love not the Lord Jesus Christ, let him be Anathema" (1 Corinthians 16:22). If I love Him as my Savior and Lord, then my plans, my time, my money, my talents, my marriage, my life-style, all will come under His sway.

A HIGH HONOR

On hearing Peter's magnificent confession Jesus pronounced a blessing on him, adding, "Thou art Peter, and upon this rock I will build my church; and the gates of hell shall not prevail against it. And I will give unto thee the keys of the kingdom of heaven: and whatsoever thou shalt bind on earth shall be bound in heaven: and whatsoever thou shalt loose on earth shall be loosed in heaven" (Matthew 16:18, 19).

The Roman Catholic church takes this statement to

mean that Jesus would build His church on Peter who would then have supreme authority over the church universal, and for all time through his successors.

But not all church leaders held to the view that Peter was the rock. Other views are mentioned in Oscar Cullman's massive study on Peter. He says, "Chrysostom explains that the rock on which Christ will build his Church means the faith of confession (*Peter,* Westminster Press, Philadelphia, 1953, p. 162). This view holds that as people confess Christ as Lord, and band together for corporate worship and service, this fellowship would never die out. The torch of faith would be passed on to succeeding generations who would hold the same confession triumphantly against all the enemies of darkness.

On the same page Cullman points out still another interpretation, "According to Augustine, Jesus meant by the rock not Peter but himself." The Reformers, too, basically believed that Jesus was the rock. They distinguish between the two words for "rock" in Jesus' declaration, "Thou art Peter (petros—little rock), and upon this rock (petra—big rock, implying Christ) I will build my church."

Peter refers to Christ as rock or stone more than once. For example, after the healing of the lame man Peter gives the credit to Jesus Christ crucified and risen, calling Him "the stone which was set at nought of you builders, which is become the head of the corner" (Acts 4:10, 11).

Also in his epistle he likens Christ to "a living stone, disallowed indeed of men, but chosen of God" (1 Peter 2:4). Then with reference to Christ Peter adds, "Wherefore also it is contained in the scripture, Behold, I lay in Sion a chief corner stone, elect, precious: and he that believeth on him shall not be confounded. Unto you therefore which believe he is precious: but unto them which be disobedient, the stone which the builders disallowed, the same is made the head of the corner, And a stone of stumbling, and a rock of offence" (2:6–8).

Cullman reaches an interesting conclusion. Based on Ephesians 2:20 and Revelation 21:14, he would make the foundation a combination of Christ and the apostles. "Jesus himself is the foundation or corner stone. . . . But this does not prevent the apostles from being the foundation composed of human instruments of God and resting in turn upon Christ; nor does it prevent Peter from having the prominent role among them" (p. 217).

Though in his view all the apostles form the foundation, Cullman holds that Peter is the most visible rock. He preached the sermons that opened the Gospel to both Jew and Gentile, a viable fulfillment of Jesus' promise to give him the keys of the kingdom. At Pentecost his message came with such conviction that 3,000 of his own nation believed. M. R. DeHaan called this the first use of the keys (Simon Peter, *Sinner and Saint,* Zondervan, 1954, p. 114). Peter's second use of the keys opened the Gospel to the Samaritans. Though Philip had conducted a great revival in Samaria, the Holy Spirit was not given them until Peter came down in person to approve (Acts 8:15–17).

Third use of the keys was his visit to Cornelius' home, just prior to which on a Joppa roof he was given a vision of unclean animals which he was commanded to eat. Says DeHaan, "Now all of this, of course, was to prepare Peter for the third use of the keys" (p. 116). After the vision, Peter was ready to accept the "unclean" Gentiles who would soon knock on his door to ask him to accompany them to the "unclean" household of Cornelius.

But to establish from Peter's use of the keys his "apostolic authority" as the bishop of Rome, and beyond that as the supreme Primate over the church universal, goes beyond scriptural evidence. The Bible never specifically says that Peter visited Rome, unless Peter used the word "Babylon" to refer cryptically to the empire's capital (1 Peter 5:13).

Extra-biblical data indicates that Peter probably came to Rome. Cullman, after thoroughly researching the literary and archeological sources, concludes that Peter arrived in Rome near the end of his life, where after a very short ministry, he died a martyr under Nero and was buried there (p. 152).

Peter's presence at Rome, even if it were a fact, plus the prominence of the church at Rome in the second and third centuries, does not prove that the primacy of the church was transferred there, much less Rome's divine right to primacy for all time. Says Cullman, "Until the beginning of the third century it never occurred to a single Bishop of Rome to refer the saying in Matthew 16:17ff to himself in the sense of leadership of the entire Church" (p. 234). No succession can be traced that leads from Jerusalem to any other city, including Rome. Nor is there any hint of succession in Jesus' promise to Peter.

Even at Jerusalem Peter's sole supremacy cannot be established. Undoubtedly he was leader in the early Jerusalem church. Peter led the election for a successor to Judas (Acts 1:15-26). Peter was the instrument of healing for the lame man and the interpreter of the miracle in the sermon that followed (Acts 3). Peter was the spokesman for the defense against the Sanhedrin on two occasions (Acts 4, 5). Peter exercised the discipline that resulted in the sudden deaths of Ananias and Sapphira (Acts 5). Peter was the instrument of miracle in the raising of Dorcas (Act 9). Peter was released from prison in answer to an all-night prayer meeting (Acts 12).

Then Peter disappears off the pages of Acts after Chapter 12, except for his testimony at the church council in Acts 15. If Peter's primacy were a fact, is it likely that

Luke would have written Peter out of the picture and given Paul the amazingly prominent role in the rest of the history of Acts?

Also, James became the leader in the Jerusalem church by the time of the first church council. It was James who gave the verdict and spoke with finality, not Peter (Acts 15:13). James was listed first among the church pillars Paul visited on his early visit to Jerusalem, with Peter mentioned second (Galatians 2:9). The expression describing Jerusalem visitors to Antioch, "certain came from James," hints at James' headship in the mother church (Galatians 2:12).

On occasions John seemed to have the ascendency. John reclined next to Jesus at the last supper, so that Peter had to relay his question to Jesus through the beloved disciple. To John, Jesus assigned the care of His mother. John was the first to recognize the risen Lord on the shore of Galilee (John 21:7).

The same authority given Peter that "whatsoever thou shalt bind (loose) on earth shall be bound (loosed) in heaven," was given to all the Twelve as well (Matthew 16:19; 18:18).

Even the naming of Peter as "the first" can be explained by literary style (Matthew 10:2). The definite article is missing in the original, so that the wording is simply "first, Peter." It is similar to someone giving a list of those on the Supreme Court by beginning, "First Justice John Doe, Justice So-and-so, etc." Employed as a cliche, this use of the word "first" creeps into our writing and speaking without any intent of giving priority or ranking. Its context is in the order of listing.

Paul never considered himself inferior to Peter. Rather he openly stated, "For I suppose I was not a whit behind the very chiefest apostles" (2 Corinthians 11:5). In fact, on one occasion Paul contradicted Peter to his face, rebuking him openly for his wrong behavior in withdrawing fellowship from Gentile believers at Antioch (Galatians 2:11–14). Apparently Paul did not consider Peter the supreme and infallible authority.

A SEVERE REPRIMAND

Not long after Peter received words of blessing and honor from the Lord he was given a strong rebuke by his Master. At one moment he was congratulated as recipient of a revelation from the heavenly Father; soon after he was called a tool of the devil. Why was commendation so soon followed by condemnation?

The reason was—Peter was correct on the Person of Christ, for which he was blessed, but he was wrong on the work of Christ, for which he was reprimanded.

Right after His prediction of a victorious church and Peter's privileged part therein, the Lord began to speak of His coming sufferings. The place—Jerusalem; the source—the religious leaders; the extent—death. Whereas a few moments earlier the theme had been the Person of Christ, the emphasis now swings to the necessity of His death.

At this point Peter took Jesus aside to rebuke Him, strongly denying such things would ever happen. He thought of Christ victorious and taking a throne with pomp and circumstance, not of Him dying. Though the Old Testament predicted a Messiah who would suffer as well as reign, most Messianic expectation dwelt on the rule and kingdom He would bring. No wiser than his countrymen, Peter would want to spare His master all such trial and affliction. Even as late as a few weeks before the crucifixion the disciples did not understand the reality of the cross (Luke 18:31–34).

Peter's denial of Jesus' sufferings drew strong reaction from the Lord, who said, in effect, "Peter, don't you recognize you are cutting at the core of the Gospel? To forgive sins I must die. Without the shedding of blood there is no remission. The path to the kingdom is by way of the cross. Without My death there will be no dominion. Don't you realize it's the devil who is prompting you to block the cross? Peter, you are repeating the same temptation I suffered from the devil when he offered me all the kingdoms of the world if I would bow down to him. Then I would not go to the cross, and all would be loss—no redemption. Peter, you are not minding the things of God, but of men!"

A SOLEMN DEMAND

Perhaps Peter tried to block out the thought of suffering on the part of Jesus because if such was his Master's destiny, what would happen to him? Jesus addressed the issue by saying that if any man would come after Him, he must take up his cross daily and follow Him (Matthew 16:24). He added, "For whosoever will save his life shall lose it: and whosoever will lose his life for my sake shall find it" (vs. 25).

Not only was Jesus determined to follow the path which led to suffering and death, undeterred by Peter's passionate objection, but also the apostles had to be willing to follow such a path, including every true follower of Christ.

When the Allies were planning the invasion of Europe in the second World War, more information was needed on enemy coastal installations. Whoever investigated these operations had to be a man of advanced scientific knowledge. This created the danger of a top British scientist falling into enemy hands. British command wanted a scientist who would be willing to be shot rather than captured. Professor Wendell volunteered. Sneaked ashore on Europe's coast, the brilliant scientist began his examination of enemy installations. All the time he worked, British soldiers had their guns pointing, but not at a potential enemy which might appear momentarily from the nearby forests. Rather, they were trained directly at the heart of Professor Wendell. He had agreed to have his life snuffed out by his own countrymen rather than become a prized enemy possession. Similarly, the Lord wants His followers to present their bodies as living sacrifices.

In this episode Peter had been confronted with the doctrine of the Person of Christ, and the doctrine of the work of Christ. He received an A+ on Christ's person, but an F on Christ's work. He needed more instruction on Christ's death on the cross. This he would receive in the experience of the transfiguration, which followed a week later.

5

Glimpse of Glory

(Matthew 17:1–8; Mark 9:1–10;
Luke 9:28–36)

A fashion fad a few years ago was a coat made of phosphorescent plastic that glowed in the dark.

On one unforgettable occasion Simon Peter saw Jesus' garments shine like the sun in the midst of darkness. Jesus had taken the inner three—Peter, James, and John—up into a mountain, probably Mt. Hermon which overlooked Caesarea Philippi where Peter had recently made his confession of faith. While Jesus was praying, the miracle of the transfiguration took place. But the three disciples were slumbering. Peter is the one specifically mentioned as drowsy. "Peter and they that were with him were heavy with sleep" (Luke 9:32).

Though not specifically stated, it was likely at night. Jesus used to spend nights on mountains. The disciples were sleeping. The transfiguration would be highlighted against a background of darkness. The record says they came down from the mountain the next day (Luke 9:37).

PETER NEEDED AN EXPERIENCE TO STRENGTHEN HIS FAITH

Jesus had recently startled His disciples by telling them He was going to suffer and die. They couldn't comprehend Deity dying. So to take the sting from His "death" announcement, Jesus promised that some of His hearers would not die till they had seen the Son of Man come with power.

Six days later (eight—according to the Hebrew custom of adding in the preceding and succeeding days) came the fulfillment of Jesus' promise to show them His glory (Matthew 17:1; Luke 9:28). The gospel writers regard the transfiguration as a dress rehearsal of the power of Jesus Christ in His coming kingdom. Peter, James, and John were the "some" who did not taste death before this foretaste of coming glory.

When He was acknowledged by Peter as the Son of God, the face of Jesus looked like the face of other men, possessing no evidence of deity or power. But now these three disciples were to behold His face transformed into sunlike brilliance.

PETER RECEIVED A PHENOMENAL EXPERIENCE

Both the face and garments of Christ became radiant. His outer cloak, called the simlah, patterned in broad stripes of black alternating with brown or white, was transformed into shining white. Mark says the garment became whiter than any earthly bleaching could make it. The effect was dazzling, perhaps like lightning flashing out against the inky night. This scene reminds us of the awesome description of the Son of Man among the churches in Revelation (1:12–15).

The Person of Christ

Christ's real self now shone through. When He came to earth, He gave up His outward splendor, but not His deity. Had He chosen, He could have walked around Palestine with His glory always radiating, flashing and shining.

The Greek word for transfiguration gives us our English *metamorphosis,* meaning a change into one's real nature. Christ assumed the outward expression of His true inward nature.

Another Greek word for *transform* means assuming an outward expression not indicative of one's inner nature, as when Satan and false apostles masquerade as angels of light. The transfiguration was no masquerade. The exterior Christ assumed did not contradict His interior nature. Christ's real essence was full of glory. His radiance came from within. It was not assumed. Intrinsic, it now broke through the veil of His humanity. This was the glory He had before the world began, which He now has at His Father's right hand, and which He will have when He returns to earth (John 17:5).

God turned Jesus inside out to show what He was really like. What if the Lord turned us inside out?

This miracle pointed up a greater wonder. The sudden shining-through of His glory was indeed a great phenomenon, but its concealment for the previous thirty years was a greater marvel. Just as the eclipse of the sun for a few minutes is startling and newsworthy, so the blocking of Christ's glory for three decades amazes us. How could a human body house God and hide His glory. Jesus was a monarch walking around in disguise, wearing rags of humanity over splended robes of royalty.

Peter and the other two were indeed strengthened by this revelation. Jesus was indeed the mighty, glorious Son of God. They had no trouble believing this, but they did wonder how One so glorious could ever possibly die. Peter had rebuked Jesus just a week before for speaking of His death. The transfiguration, a confirmation of the person of Christ, was a corrective to Peter's erroneous view of His work. The rest of the drama would make the cross more understandable.

The Heavenly Visitors

As the disciples' eyes became accustomed to the brightness, two more figures appeared, who in some way were recognized as Moses and Elijah, and heard conversing with Jesus. Such a scene confirmed their confidence in life beyond the grave. Moses had died fourteen centuries before, and Elijah nine. Now they were alive, and talking with each other.

More than this, these two famous Old Testament characters recognized each other, despite the fact that they had lived 500 years apart. Moses and Elijah had never met on earth, but now had been together for centuries in heaven.

Also, the three disciples, who had never seen Moses nor Elijah, knew them. This episode assured Peter, James, and John of a positive answer to the oft-asked question, "Will we know each other in heaven?" What a day when we all gather together with Moses, Elijah, David, Samuel, and all the Old Testament saints, plus Peter, James, and John, and all the New Testament believers.

But even more enlightening was the topic of conversation between these Old Testament characters and Jesus. They talked about Jesus' death (decease) which was soon to happen in Jerusalem (Luke 9:31). This was the very matter for which Peter had recently rebuked Jesus. Now Peter learned that the death of Jesus was of vital interest to the two leading Old Testament representatives.

The Old Testament is often summed up under "the Law and the Prophets." Moses was the leading person in connection with the law, and Elijah the outstanding prophet. So the two men who appeared with Jesus typified full Old Testament homage to Jesus' coming death in Jerusalem. Perhaps in the transfiguration conversation Moses spoke of the Passover lamb, or the brazen serpent being lifted up in the wilderness. Elijah might have mentioned one of the Messianic prophecies. In the upper room on that first Easter night Christ showed from the Law and the Prophets how He had to suffer and be raised.

Had the leaders of Jesus' day been in harmony with Moses, they would have accepted Christ. If Moses and Elijah could somehow have attended the trial of Jesus as witnesses, they would have testified in His behalf. By rejecting Jesus, the Sanhedrin placed itself outside the successors of Moses and Elijah.

At the manifestation of Christ's greatest glory the heavenly visitors spoke of His deepest humiliation. With His head bathed in glory they talked of His head crowned with thorns. With His garments glistening with celestial beauty they talked of the occasion when they would be gambled for by Roman soldiers.

The transfiguration involved a combination of suffering and glory, a blending of a suffering Lamb with a reign in dominion and power. Peter never forgot the union of cross and crown. The indelible impression is reflected in his frequent linking of the two in his writings. For example, he spoke of prophets who "testified beforehand the sufferings of Christ, and the glory that should follow" (1 Peter 1:11). See also 1 Peter 4:13; 5:1).

Peter's Thoughtless Recommendation

As Moses and Elijah faded from the scene, impetuous Peter felt he had to say something, so blurted out, "Master, it's good to be here. Let us make three booths, one for you, and one for Moses, and one for Elijah." His suggestion was ill-advised. Perhaps in his preoccupation with a suffering Christ Peter wished to capture Christ in His transfigured state. No huts were needed for Moses or Elijah in their heavenly existence. Imagine these six personages living on a mountain-top when down below squalor reigned among men who so badly needed the touch of Christ. The kingdom had not yet come.

Once again Peter had opened his mouth too quickly. The Gospels, in recording Peter's poor, babbling words, indicate he really did not know what he said. Had such temples been built and survived, they would have become shrines to which people would have made pilgrimages from all over the world. Peter's pointless reaction is reflected in this stanza,

> *"My willing soul would stay*
> *In such a frame as this,*
> *And sit and sing itself away*
> *To everlasting bliss."*

The Father's Voice

While Peter was still mouthing his ill-timed advice, a bright cloud overshadowed them, which some think was the Shekinah. As the cloud approached and enveloped them, they fell on their faces, prostrate with fear. Then came a voice from the cloud, "This is my beloved Son; hear ye him."

The Father's voice rebuked Peter's proposal. "Don't put my beloved Son on the same level with Moses and Elijah by building tabernacles for them all. Let Moses and Elijah go. They are just servants. The Law and the Prophets are fulfilled in my Son. Hear His words." Three times during Christ's ministry a heavenly voice attested to His Sonship (Matthew 3:17; 17:5; John 12:28).

Dire Need in the Valley

After giving the Sermon on the Mount, our Lord came down to heal a leper. Here, after the Mount of Transfiguration experience, He descended to the ugly scene of a demon-possessed, frothing-at-the-mouth, screaming, stumbling lad. An only child, loved by his father, he was now healed by the Only Begotten Son of God, Who was also beloved by His Father.

How often we experience some mountain-top delight: a Sunday service, a prayer meeting, a missionary report, a Bible conference, an evangelistic crusade, a small Bible study. But we cannot remain there. Down in the valley of our own neighborhood are people with desperate needs. How selfish to bask in the sunlight of divine privileges, and fail to go down with Christ to the crowded ways of life.

PETER DIDN'T PUT HIS EXPERIENCE ABOVE THE SCRIPTURES

Peter, James, and John needed this mountain-top revelation. For a week they had been in gloom because of their Master's prediction of His coming sufferings and death. Now the darkness had been somewhat dispelled. Though the Lord would die, He would die as the Lord of glory.

What an experience! They had glimpsed a bit of the glory of the Eternal Son of God. They had heard two outstanding Old Testament characters freely talk with Christ on His coming death. They had heard the voice of the Heavenly Father commending His Son, and commanding the apostles' attention to His words. They had foretasted the blessedness of communing in heaven with all the saints of all the ages and with Christ.

The transfiguration helped James face a martyr's death when he was beheaded not long after the stoning of Stephen (Acts 12:1). John referred to the transfiguration in his Gospel's prologue, "And the Word was made flesh, and dwelt among us, (and we beheld his glory, the glory as of the only begotten of the Father,) full of grace and truth" (1:14).

Peter could never forget the glory of it all. Thirty years later he penned this report, "For we have not followed cunningly devised fables, when we made known unto you the power and coming of our Lord Jesus Christ, but were eyewitnesses of his majesty. For he received from God the Father honour and glory, when there came such a voice to him from the excellent glory, This is my beloved Son, in whom I am well pleased. And this voice which came from heaven we heard, when we were with him in the holy mount" (2 Peter 1:16–18).

However, tremendous as was this experience, Peter then turns his readers to something even more certain—the Word of God. He immediately advances from the sensory data of the transfiguration to the firm word of written revelation. Glorious as was the light that shone through the Savior's face and garments, more certain is the light of the Word of God. Peter declares, "We have also a more sure word of prophecy; whereunto ye do well that ye take heed, as unto a light that shineth in a dark place, until the day dawn, and the day star arise in your hearts: Knowing this first, that no prophecy of the scripture is of any private interpretation. For the prophecy came not in old time by the will of man: but holy men of God spake as they were moved by the Holy Ghost" (2 Peter 1:19–21).

Today's generation, enamored with experientialism, seems to prefer subjective experience to objective truth. Feelings take precedence over biblical facts. "I had this experience. It changed my life, so it must be right. You cannot take it away from me." But Peter says that even his most sensational experience of seeing the transfigured Christ in conversation with Moses and Elijah must take second place to the sure Word of Scripture. Personal experience must bow to the authority of the Bible.

Experience by itself cannot lead us to truth because it is incomplete, fragmentary, subjective, and relative, depending on our particular bias or viewpoint. Organ music, stained glass windows, and a formal prayer, might move some deeply, while turning others off.

A young man was watching an Easter sunrise service on television. Suddenly, as the speaker exclaimed, "He is risen," the rising sun shone through the window and reflected brightly back into the young man's face. Said the youth, "I knew at that moment that Christ had risen from the dead." But the truth of the resurrection cannot be established by any such experience of sudden sunshine. Rather, we must go to the Word of God to find it.

When we place experience over truth, we have no defense against those who claim they have experienced the solution to life's problems in TM, Hare Krishna, or some other eastern religion. At a meeting with international students on a college campus, when one Christian spoke of his joy and peace as a Christian, a Moslem student asserted that he found joy and peace in the Islamic faith. Experience does not lead to the royal road of truth. In the final analysis, the truth of Christianity is what counts, not just heartwarming experience.

Even valid experiences among Christians do not set the standard for truth. One preacher refused to have his biography written lest readers consider his Christian experience to be the norm for all believers. One danger of pushing experience is that often weak Christians worry when their experience doesn't measure up to the one just presented. For example, a new Christian, hearing an older one say that from the moment of his conversion years before he has never had a single doubt as to the reality of his salvation, and realizing that in his few short months as a professing Christian he already has had several periods of serious doubt as to his forgiveness, began to worry again over the genuineness of his salvation.

Some are led to expect warm glows, or binding flashes.

But no Bible verse ever says that the believer will see light-ning, feel warm, or suffer electric shock.

Another danger of promoting experience is that of a strong personality trying to force his particular experience on others as the norm, even hinting that without it others have not fully arrived. A deacon in a Canadian church, whose conversion had been preceded by months of convic-tion, groveling in distress by the base of a riverside pier, thought that everybody coming before the deacons' board to give testimony with a view to church membership should have had the same experience. His pastor had to gently remind him that, though Christ was the only way to God, others experienced different ways of coming to Him.

Someone imagined a conversation between two blind men who had been healed by Jesus. One told how Jesus touched him. The other interrupted, "Jesus touched me twice because the first time I saw men only as trees walking. If He touched you only once, I don't think you really got healed." He went out and started the *Two-Touch Church,* leaving the other fellow to rally supporters for his *One-Touch Chapel.*

Peter never urged the other nine disciples to seek a transfiguration experience. He didn't say, "If you haven't seen Moses and Elijah, you should doubt you're in the king-dom." In fact, the privileged three were told to keep it quiet till after the resurrection.

A man asked a preacher if he had ever talked in tongues since becoming a Christian. When the preacher said no, the layman said, "That practice is a valid New Testament experience. How can you teach others when you are short on experience?"

The preacher replied, "Is raising the dead a valid New Testament experience?" When the layman said yes, the preacher asked, "Have you ever raised anyone from the dead?" The layman had to admit he hadn't, also that he had never walked on water, nor changed water into wine, all valid New Testament experiences. The layman was setting up Christian experience as the norm, while failing to rightly divide the word of truth.

John R. W. Stott says the "revelation of the purpose of God in Scripture should be sought primarily in its *didactic* rather than its *descriptive* parts. More precisely, we should look for it in the teaching of Jesus, and in the sermons and writings of the apostles, rather than in the purely narrative portions of Acts. What is described in Scripture as having happened to others is not necessarily intended for us, whereas what is promised to us we are to appropriate, and what is commanded us we are to obey" (Baptism & Fulness, *The Work of the Holy Spirit Today,* p. 15, Intervarsity Press, 1976).

We do need to put the teaching of God's word into practice. Word and experience should be wedded so that we are doers of the Word, not hearers only. But doctrine must travel from the Bible to experience, and not from experience to the Bible. One's experience cannot be made normative for all.

For example, an unbeliever becomes seriously ill and nearly dies. In those critical moments, he sees beautiful sights and hears lovely music. Musing after recovery, he deduces that he had a glimpse of heaven, so must be headed there when he dies. But he cannot build his hope on that experience, for the Bible promises no hope of heaven to the unbeliever, but rather condemnation.

Even a believer in Christ who sees celestial creatures and hears rapturous music in near-fatal illness cannot base his guarantee of heaven on that experience. Though his experience may have been true—he may actually have had a foretaste of heaven—his confidence of heaven must be grounded on the Word of God which says, "He that hath the Son hath life."

According to Jesus' story, the rich man in hell wanted Abraham to send Lazarus to warn his five brothers lest they come to the same place of torment. But Abraham said, "They have Moses and the prophets: let them hear them." The rich man suggested that if someone came back from the dead to give a warning his brothers would repent. But Abraham replied, "If they hear not Moses and the prophets, neither will they be persuaded, though one rose from the dead" (Luke 16:27–31). Jesus said, in effect, the Word of God is more powerful than experience, even the experience of being warned by someone back from the grave.

The early church didn't turn the world topsy-turvy by preaching titillating experiences, but by centering on the proclamation of the Gospel. Peter preached, not about his episode of walking on the water, nor the transfiguration, but Christ crucified and risen. Paul preached, not his exciting noon-day Damascus Road conversion, but the person and work of Christ. He customarily opened the Scriptures to show how Christ fulfilled Old Testament prophecies by dying for our sins and rising. Examination of sermons, or the substance of sermons in Acts, shows all centered on the cross and resurrection of Christ, not on the experiences of the apostolic leaders. The two recorded times Paul recited his conversion story involved his defense, first before his countrymen who had just beaten him, and second, before Agrippa.

Encounter with truth should lead to an experience of deliverance and growth. Faith without works is dead. But experience may cause us to drift hopelessly on the sea of subjective whim, unless anchored to the sure word of prophecy.

6

Questions Peter Asked

Children can ask the profoundest questions, such as, "Why did the angels walk up Jacob's ladder if they had wings?" Or, "What does the wind do when it's not blowing?"

Adults often refrain from asking questions lest they reveal their ignorance. "If I keep quiet, people may think me dumb. But if I open my mouth, they'll know it!" Not so with children who make no pretense of false knowledge but blurt their queries right out, unhibited and unembarrassed.

Peter never hesitated to voice questions. A man of transparent sincerity, without hypocrisy, cunning, deception or diplomacy, he took a straight line on any matter he didn't understand. Irrepressible, his openness spilled over into his speech, making him talkative by nature, and sometimes the victim of "foot-in-mouth" disease.

Perhaps this childlike quality of always asking questions helped endear Peter to Jesus Who one day set a child in the midst, telling His disciples to become like it. But whether in childlike humility or in rash impetuosity, Peter was always the first to ask Jesus questions. At times he may have been representing his friends. Chrysostom called him "the mouthpiece of the disciples."

Approximately a dozen of his questions have been recorded, including some rhetorical, indirect, implied, or those stemming from curiosity. They fall into three general areas:

those relating to the start of the Christian life, those having to do with service along the Christian life, and those pertaining to the future.

QUESTIONS RELATING TO THE START OF THE CHRISTIAN LIFE

The first question deals with the depravity of human nature, thus showing the need for new life.

Question 1 "Then answered Peter and said unto him, Declare unto us this parable" (Matthew 15:15). In effect, Peter is saying, "What does this parable mean?"

Our Lord's redemptive dealing with us goes right to the root of our sinful nature. One day He gave a parabolic illustration, "Not that which goeth into the mouth defileth a man, but that which cometh out of the mouth, this defileth a man" (Matthew 15:11). A little later Peter asked the meaning of this saying.

In Jewish tradition, before a man could eat, he was required to wash his hands in a prescribed way, as a ritual, not for cleanliness. Jesus explained that it was not what went into the mouth that made a man unclean, but what came up from the mind and spirit defiled the actions of life. Then He listed examples of thoughts, words, and deeds that find their origin in the heart. "For out of the heart proceed evil thoughts, murders, adulteries, fornications, thefts, false witness, blasphemies" (vs. 19). Then He added, "These are the things which defile a man: but to eat with unwashen hands defileth not a man (vs. 20).

Basically, man is mean, ornery, deceitful, and depraved. He needs a radical change to make him giving instead of grasping, and sacrificial instead of selfish. When a church in Hartford, Conn., needed several thousand dollars for an outreach program, its minister took out a personal loan of $20,000 to lend to people who would "multiply" the money for Christ, as people did in the parable of the talents. Out of thousands of applicants who responded to his widely publicized appeals, he selected fifty. The project turned out to be a flop by the minister's own admission. Only five people returned any money whatsoever, leaving him with $18,000 to repay the bank out of his own pocket. Nearly half the recipients gave phoney names and addresses and couldn't be found. Most of the others never used the money for the creative ideas they outlined, but spent it on themselves. When the minister tried to collect from these folks, including several business leaders who took $1,000 loans, he heard such remarks as "Get lost," or "Perhaps I'll pay you back some day" (Christianity Today, Editorial, 8 June 1979, p. 13).

Besides showing the need for wisdom in church financing, the incident illustrates the biblical doctrine of man's sinfulness. A sign over an out-of-order clock read, "Don't blame my hands. The trouble lies deeper."

The Gospel of Christ goes to the root of the trouble. Man's inner nature can be regenerated by the Spirit of God. The Lion of the tribe of Judah, by His sacrifice on the cross as the incarnate Lamb of God, can conquer the tiger of man's fallen nature. The source of this new life is the subject of another of Peter's questions.

Question 2 "To whom shall we go?" (John 6:68).

When the day after feeding the 5,000, the crowd wanted to make Him king, Jesus decided to make clear to the multitude that His kingdom was not political, but spiritual. He urged them to labor, not for the meat that perishes, but for the bread which endures eternally. When He told them He was the Bread sent down from heaven which they must eat, his hearers puzzled, murmured, and argued over the meaning of His teaching. Many professing disciples said, "This is a hard saying; who can hear it?," then turned their backs on Him and walked away. Looking around to the Twelve who had just seen the fabric of His popularity shattered, Jesus asked pathetically, "Will ye also go away?" In effect, "They have no appetite for my message. Will you also leave and make it unanimous?"

Then came a beautiful, though rhetorical question from Peter, "Lord, to whom shall we go? thou hast the words of eternal life. And we believe and are sure that thou art that Christ, the Son of the living God" (vv. 68, 69).

We need to go somewhere. Sooner or later in life it dawns on us gradually or joltingly that we cannot cope with all the problems of existence by ourselves. An inner craving for the eternal makes us as fretful as a child suddenly awakened in an empty room.

Alienated from God through sin, we ask, "How shall we ever stand accepted before a righteous God. To whom shall we go for forgiveness? Where do we go in loneliness, illness, pain, old age, the valley of the shadow of death, or in the dark periods of life when the lights on which we counted are turned out, leaving no stars nor sun for many days?"

Sooner or later, with slow or crushing force, we discover that we must go somewhere outside of self to find the satisfying bread and the living water.

Shall we turn to money? But money cannot buy health, happiness, nor a home in heaven. Fame, pleasure, and power are likewise useless. Neither can stained glass windows, liturgy, nor candles, quench the soul's fervor for God.

Shall we go to education? Education can enlighten the mind, but cannot satisfy the soul nor control man's sinful nature. Man misuses almost every gadget his brain invents. Our moral brakes do not match our mental horsepower.

Can we turn to sociologists, philosophers, politicians, or to religious leaders like Confucius, Buddha, or Mohammed, none of whom ever emerged from the grave? Can we turn to the rulers of our countries or to the United Nations to satisfy the deepest longings of the human heart?

How about science, which has given us so many marvelous inventions? During his sermon a London preacher said, "A lady in our congregation has lost her son. She wants to know where he has gone. She asks if there is any balm for her sorrow. Or any word that can give her hope of reunion beyond the grave." Then he called out, "Science, can you give us the answer?" Silence followed. After a few minutes he lifted his Bible, "The Word of God gives us the only answer to these questions. Jesus Christ has the words of eternal life."

No alternative to Christ exists. An agnostic, visiting another agnostic on his deathbed, encouraged him by saying, "Stick to it, fellow." But the other replied weakly, "There's nothing to stick to." Christ is superior by virtue of His words, works, and worth.

None ever spake like this Man. His matchless words have accorded Him the title of *The Teacher.* His teachings have stood the test of time, and are more up-to-date than the latest psychology text.

Who can rival His miracles? Who else can still the storm, feed the multitude, cast out our demons, or raise the dead?

No one ever convicted Him of sin. No guile ever proceeded from His lips. His character was flawless, his goodness unassailable. Offering up that stainless life as a spotless Lamb, He paid the price for our forgiveness and adoption into the family of God. Because of His resurrection, death is no leap in the dark. So, Christ gives life abundant here by granting guidance, strength, and purpose, and likewise answers the problem of existence beyond the grave.

So, when others who had been following for material profit and without spiritual discernment turned away, Peter said, in effect, "No, Lord, we're not going away. We're staying right here. You are the answer to life."

This salvation, found only through Christ and effecting a change right at the root of man's moral nature, must be appropriated by personal faith. The matter of individual appropriation is involved in another of Peter's questions.

Question 3 "Master, the multitude throng thee and press thee, and sayest thou, Who touched me?" (Luke 8:45).

One day when a crowd was pressing around Jesus, a woman, suffering a twelve-year blood disease which doctors could not cure, touched the hem of His garment and was immediately healed. When Jesus asked who it was that touched Him, Peter asked this question, in effect, "With everyone crowding You, how can You ask if anyone touched You?"

But Jesus knew someone had touched Him with the intensity of faith. It's possible to be among the crowd worshiping in the Sunday morning service, or attending the evangelistic crusade, and yet be without faith in Christ. Many were thronging Christ, but only one had the faith to touch Him.

Investigation of a fire-fighting system in place in a Texas hospital for 35 years, with complete reliance on it for the safety of patients and building, revealed no connection had ever been made with the water-main. The connecting pipe in the system ended a few feet from the main pipe. Fortunately, no fire had ever occurred. Naturally, hurried action was taken to complete the connection.

Just as no one can eat for you, sleep for you, or get married for you, so no one can receive forgiveness for you. It's a personal matter. Like the sick woman who touched

Jesus, so you, realizing the sinfulness of your heart, and convinced of the sufficiency of Christ, must reach out in faith to receive all the blessing that comes from the Water of Life.

QUESTIONS RELATING TO SERVICE ALONG THE CHRISTIAN WAY

The first question in this series deals with a Christian's obligation to pay taxes.

Question 4 "What about paying the temple-tax?" (Matthew 17:25).

This question was only in Peter's mind. He never got to ask it openly. One day in Capernaum, home town then of Jesus as well as of Peter, a collector of temple-taxes confronted Peter, "Doth not your master pay tribute?" Peter answered in the affirmative, knowing Jesus had paid it in the past and would pay it now.

When Peter found Jesus, he was about to ask him about paying the tax, even wondering, "Where will we get the money? You know our funds are low." But Jesus anticipated Peter's unspoken question by asking, "What thinkest thou, Simon? of whom do the kings of the earth take custom or tribute? of their own children, or of strangers?" (Matthew 17:25). Jesus' question implied His unique relationship with God as compared to other people. He is the Son; others are but subjects. Therefore He should not have to pay tax. But lest His liberty cause stumbling to others, Jesus said to pay.

Jesus' resources were so limited that He had nowhere to lay His head, and was now likely staying at Peter's house (vs. 25). Peter had left all to follow Jesus, forsaking boats and business. Jesus' next words must have given Peter hope,

"Go thou to the sea, and cast an hook, and take up the fish that first cometh up; and when thou hast opened his mouth, thou shalt find a piece of money: that take, and give unto them for me and thee" (vs. 27).

With wonder Peter must have taken his line and gone fishing. Sure enough, in the mouth of the first fish he caught was a stater, a coin that equaled two half-shekels in value, the exact amount needed to pay the temple-tax for Jesus and Peter. Though this was the only miracle performed by the Lord for His own benefit, it also profited Peter, who must have been profoundly impressed by our Lord's perfect knowledge of the whereabouts of a fish that had sometime previously caught a glittering coin which had been dropped overboard by some fisherman, child or passenger, and which was the exact amount needed.

What is the Christian viewpoint on paying taxes? Some say avoid paying taxes at any cost because the government wastes money with its bureaucrats in Washington and all the welfare fraud. A fine line exists between tax avoidance and tax evasion. An estimated 50 billion dollars a year in taxes is lost in tax evasion. Though government waste and excesses are not to be condoned, nevertheless believers should pay their taxes willingly, at the same time exercising their responsibility to influence government to be more efficient.

Peter never forgot his Master's command to respect authority. Though Peter always put obedience to God above obedience to man, even if it meant arrest and imprisonment (Acts 4:18–20), he was careful to instruct his readers, "Submit yourselves to every ordinance of man for the Lord's sake: whether it be to the king, as supreme; Or unto governors, as unto them that are sent by him for the punishment of evildoers, and for the praise of them that do well. For so is the will of God, that with well doing ye may put to silence the ignorance of foolish men" (1 Peter 2:13–17).

Question 5 "How oft shall my brother sin against me, and I forgive him? till seven times?" (Matthew 18:21)

Peter's suggestion of forgiveness seven times instead of the rabbinical teaching of three showed how far Peter had grown under Jesus' teachings. But he did not anticipate the celestial arithmetic of forgiveness contained in Jesus' answer—"until 70 times 7." Peter, who would stand in need of great forgiveness after his denial of Christ, never forgot the parable of the merciless servant which Jesus immediately gave to illustrate His command to forgive 70 times 7.

In this story the Lord used exaggeration to drive home the necessity of a forgiving spirit. About to be tossed into prison, a servant who owed his master a staggering debt of roughly 20 million dollars begged for mercy and received it. But then the forgiven servant on his release refused a plea for mercy from a fellow servant who owed him a tiny debt of 20 dollars, and threw him into jail. Whereupon the master who had at first remitted the 20-million-dollar debt reversed his initial cancellation and threw the merciless servant into jail. Jesus ended the parable, "So likewise shall my heavenly Father do also unto you, if ye from your hearts forgive not every one his brother their trespasses" (Matthew 18:35).

The refusal of the merciless servant to exercise mercy revealed his failure to realize the enormity of his debt, and his lack of appreciation of the vastness of the mercy extended him.

Our trespasses against Christ are a million times greater than the few wrongs of any human against us. If we genuinely ask forgiveness from Christ for our immense debt, how can we refuse mercy to a fellow-believer whose sin against us is miniscule by comparison. A refusal to forgive underscores a lack of comprehension of Christ's grace. An unforgiving spirit reflects an unforgiven spirit. Since Calvary opened the floodgates of unlimited mercy, he who is forgiven much should certainly love much.

A man retorted, "I'll forgive him this time but never again!" What if Christ said the same to the forgiver.

A woman told her pastor, "I'll forgive Mrs. X., but I won't have anything to do with her. I don't want to see her again. I won't let her in my house!" The pastor replied, "Suppose Christ treated you the same way, would have nothing more to do with you, nor ever let you into His heavenly home?"

How often people react, "I'll forgive, but I won't forget." Christ has both forgiven and forgotten our sins against Him. To remember a grievance by holding a grudge indicates a lack of full forgiveness. If we forgive, we must forget.

A wife found it difficult to speak with her unfaithful but genuinely repentant husband. This woman, with several small children, was advised to forgive and forget, not to be proud or stubborn, but to take him back. She took the advice. She reported that the eight years that followed were their happiest, noting that her husband had recently died. The warmth of their last years together would sustain her forever, she said.

Peter learned well the lesson of forgiveness. This is why he wrote, "Not rendering evil for evil, or railing for railing: but contrariwise blessing; knowing that ye are thereunto called, that ye should inherit a blessing (1 Peter 3:9).

Question 6 "We have forsaken all, and followed thee; what shall we have therefore?" (Matthew 19:27)

When the rich, young ruler, unable to pay the price of discipleship by giving up all His possessions, turned away sorrowfully from Jesus, Peter interrupted the Master's disappointment with the above question. "What do we get out of following You? Surely we'll receive some compensation for giving up our boats and business, and for the sacrifices involved in following you."

Note that Jesus did not squelch Peter by calling his motive unworthy. Though love is undoubtedly the noblest motive, the Lord here gave an answer that appealed to the motive of reward. First, He promised that they would sit on twelve thrones judging the twelve tribes of Israel. Second, those who gave up houses, family, or lands for His name's sake, would receive an hundredfold in this life, and in the world to come life everlasting (Matthew 19:28,29).

Most people consider themselves fortunate to get a 10 percent return on their investment. If you could double your principal, it would be a 100 percent. But to get a hundredfold dividend, this is a 10,000 percent profit. And this is what Jesus promised Peter—a hundredfold in this life.

A young man who left home to answer the call of God in an itinerant ministry testified that homes opened to him all over the country, that parents became mothers and fathers to him, and their children became brothers and sisters. He said, "I received, as Christ said, houses, brothers, sisters, mothers, and lands." He found all this, and heaven too.

A missionary broken in health after a lifetime of fruitful missionary service came home to America. On the same boat was Teddy Roosevelt, returning from a hunting expedition in Africa. At the dock in New York City big crowds gathered to see Roosevelt. Bands played. Thousands cheered. The missionary was excited to be a part of the celebration. But then his heart dropped as he realized no one had come to greet him. He went alone to a little room on the east side, where he began to complain, "Oh, Lord, I served you so faithfully all those years, and no one met me when I came home." A voice seemed to say, "You're not home yet!"

In the day of rewards many will doubtless say, "Why was I so self-centered? Why didn't I devote myself and my substance more to Jesus Christ and His work?" Why did I hesitate to make an investment that would have yielded a maximum return?"

QUESTIONS RELATING TO THE FUTURE

The Bible says there's a time to speak and a time to be silent. Peter hadn't learned the latter. Four of his questions arose from curiosity about the future, two of them regarding Jesus' immediate future, one relative to John's fate, and one to the Second Coming of the Master.

Question 7 "Who is it that betrays the Lord?" (John 13:24)

When in the upper room Jesus told the disciples that one of their number would betray Him, they questioned among themselves as to which one would do this thing, even asking Him one by one, Is it I?" (Mark 14:19). But Peter was much more inquisitive. So he beckoned to the one next to Jesus, likely John, to ask Jesus who the betrayer was. John put Peter's question directly to Jesus, "Lord, who is it?"

Jesus answered, "The one I give a sop, after I've dipped it." Then Jesus dipped the sop and gave it to Judas.

Question 8 "Lord, whither goest thou?" (John 13:36)

With Judas gone, Jesus could speak more freely. In the atmosphere of love He proceeded to prepare His disciples for what would seem to them a great tragedy. But He called it just the opposite, stating, "Now is the Son of man glorified" (vs. 31). Though Christ's glorification would include His resurrection, ascension, and exaltation at the Father's right hand, John seems to apply the term here to His death.

Addressing His disciples with a term of endearment, "little children," Jesus said, "Whither I go, ye cannot come" (vs. 33). Though they did not understand what He meant, they did comprehend the need to love. When left behind, their radical differences of temperament and smoldering jealousies would destroy their unity unless some cohesive force unified them. Hence He immediately issued a new commandment, "That ye love one another." This love would be the badge of discipleship and the basis of unity (vs. 34,35).

Concluding that Jesus was about to undertake some dangerous trip on earth, Peter asked, "Lord, whither goest thou?" Jesus replied to the effect that though Peter (and the rest) could not go with Him now, he was promised that he would be able to follow later.

After announcing His coming separation, Jesus spoke words of comfort and cheer in what is known as His farewell discourse (John 14–16). Interestingly, this message was interrupted three times by questions. Thomas, Philip, and Judas (not Iscariot) were the interrogators (14:5,8,22). Did the example of Peter, who asked the first question, encourage them to likewise ask questions?

Question 9 "Lord, and what shall this man (John) do?" (John 21:21)

After the miraculous catch of 153 fish on the Sea of Galilee, the breakfast prepared by Jesus on the shore, and the threefold affirmation of his love for the Lord, Jesus took Peter aside and told him how he was going to die.

Content after a warm breakfast, contemplating the joy of renewed fellowship and the renewed commission to "feed my sheep," Peter's calm was suddenly shattered with this prediction, "Verily, verily, I say unto thee, When thou wast young, thou girdest thyself, and walkedst wither thou wouldest: but when thou shalt be old, thou shalt stretch forth thy hands, and another shall gird thee, and carry thee whither thou wouldest not." John adds, "This spake he, signifying by what death he should glorify God. And when he had spoken this, he saith unto him, Follow me" (21:18,19). Peter would die by crucifixion.

Most people would be quite disturbed to learn years in advance just how they were going to die, so God in His mercy has drawn a curtain over such information. Peter must have been somewhat dismayed. As he walked aside with Jesus, Peter turned about and saw "the disciple whom Jesus loved" (doubtless John) following. So Peter asked, in effect, "What's going to happen to my buddy? How will his end come?"

How human to make comparisons. Why do I suffer with this illness, and not my neighbor? Why don't I get the recognition my classmate gets? Why does that deacon have a nicer and newer home? That church sends its pastor and wife to the mission field. How does that lady get her articles published? That couple will have such a good retirement fund.

The Lord doesn't want us making such comparisons. He replied to Peter, "If I will that he tarry till I come, what is that to thee? follow thou me" (vs. 22). Edith Schaeffer explains, "Jesus did not tell Peter that all the stresses and strains would balance out. He did not say that because He is perfect love and perfect justice, each of His children would have equal experience. Jesus said, in effect: 'If John is to live until I come back a second time, that is none of your affair: you are to follow my plan for your life. You, Peter, are to love me enough to trust me and follow me wherever that following leads, even to martyrdom for God's glory' " (Christianity Today, 6 December 1974, p. 32).

Jesus' reply was misreported to mean that John would not die but live till Jesus' Second Coming. But Jesus had

only said, "If John is to live till My return, what is that
to you?" In effect, "Don't make a comparison between John
and you. The real comparison to make is between what
I command you and what you do in response to my command. Your job is to follow me."

We too easily stick our nose into other peoples' Christian lives, concentrating on their successes, feats, fame, for-
tunes, and excitements, and neglecting to follow the
directions the Lord has given us. Our task is not to mind
about John, but to follow Christ.

Question 10 "Lord, speakest thou this parable unto us, or
even to all?" (Luke 12:41)

Four names, those of Peter, James, John, and Andrew,
are attached to the question as to the sign of Christ's Second
Coming and the end of the world (Mark 13:3). Jesus' answer
is known as the Olivet Discourse, rich in teaching on prophecy. This chapter deals only with questions asked by Peter,
though unnamed others may have joined in the query.

Peter did ask a question relating to the Second Coming
of Christ. It was after this teaching. "Blessed are those servants, whom the lord when he cometh shall find watching:
verily I say unto you, that he shall gird himself, and make
them to sit down to meat, and will come forth and serve
them. And if he shall come in the second watch, or come
in the third watch, and find them so, blessed are those servants. And this know, that if the goodman of the house
had known what hour the thief would come, he would have
watched, and not have suffered his house to be broken
through. Be ye therefore ready also: for the Son of man
cometh at an hour when ye think not" (Luke 12:37–40).

At this point Peter piped up, "Lord, speakest thou this
parable unto us, or even to all?" The Lord's answer left

the matter quite open, implying that this parable is for every steward in the household of faith, whether or not called to a position of leadership like the apostles.

An eastern household was ruled by a master who delegated much authority to a steward, or manager, who was responsible for the administration of the household. If in the absence of his master, a steward became careless, beat the servants, and caroused, he would have been considered unfaithful, and dealt with by his master on his return. On the other hand, faithful servants would have been given greater authority.

No man lives to himself. All believers are in some sense managers of the household of God, called to minister to each other through our God-given spiritual gifts. Faithfulness in the Master's absence will bring blessedness in the day of His return; infidelity will be punished.

At a ministers' meeting, the host pastor asked everyone present, one by one, "Do you think Jesus will come today?" Every preacher replied, "No, I think not." After going the round of the room, the host pastor solemnly repeated, "Therefore be ye also ready: for in such an hour as ye think not the Son of man cometh" (Matthew 24:44).

Matthew Henry said, "Thank God for Peter. He was always asking questions."

7

Gospel of the Basin

(John 13:1–17)

Lord Mountbatten, British military hero killed in 1979 by Irish terrorists, was given an imperial funeral service in Westminster Abbey. Indisputably, he was a courageous and gallant figure. Yet biographers described him as a very proud man. All his life he relished the spotlight and the rewards that accompanied his fame. With flambuoyance he wore ten rows of medals and decorations, including Knight Companion of the Most Noble Order of the Garter. He composed his own entry in the British "Who's Who," taking more than 1,000 words. He once said, "I am the most conceited man I have ever known."

In opposition to such arrogance the Lord Jesus Christ humbled Himself. One graphic illustration of His condescension was washing the disciples' feet the night before He died.

In first century Jewish culture common courtesy required a host, upon the arrival of his guests, to wash their feet so easily soiled by the dusty streets. This service was sometimes performed as guests reclined at the table, leaning on their left side, with their right hand free to feed themselves, head toward the table, and feet stretched out behind. A servant had easy access to the guests' feet without disturbing the meal.

Because this upper room was loaned to Jesus and the Twelve, and servants were busy elsewhere with Passover preparations, no one was available to handle the customary gesture of hospitality. However, the owner had thoughtfully provided basin, pitcher, water, and towel.

But who would do the honors? Such humble service was the farthest thought from the minds of the disciples. Amazing as it may seem, the disciples began to argue among themselves over who would have the chief places in the coming kingdom. How inappropriate when within twenty-four hours He Who was very Life would die the ignominious death reserved for aliens, slaves, and criminals.

This was the third recorded occasion of similar internal dissension (Mark 9:33,34; 10:37–41: Luke 22:24). Our Lord again patiently admonished them, saying, "he that is greatest among you, let him be as the younger; and he that is chief, as he that doth serve. For whether is greater, he that sitteth at meat, or he that serveth? is not he that sitteth at meat? but I am among you as he that serveth" (Luke 22:26,27).

In this atmosphere charged with feverish ambition no contending leader would abdicate his throne of aspiration to kneel before his subjects. With studied indifference, every disciple looked in the other direction from the towel, pitcher and basin, regarding this as task beneath dignity.

At this point, according to some harmonizers of the four Gospels, an amazing thing happened. Jesus rose from His place, discarded His outer garment, tied the towel around His waist, leaving both hands free to handle pitcher and basin, then performed the servant's chore.

When Booker T. Washington was president of a school in Alabama, a wealthy woman, not recognizing him as he walked down the street, yelled to him, "Hey, you, come in here and chop some wood."

Booker immediately turned into her yard, doffed his coat, chopped wood and carried it into the house. As he left, a servant-girl recognized the school president and told her mistress. The horrified woman hurried out to apologize.

"It's entirely all right, Madam," the great black leader replied, "I delight to do favors for my friends."

Learning an unforgettable lesson, the lady became one of the strongest financial supporters of the school.

When the Lord of Glory chose the servant's place, taking the soiled feet of the disciples in His own hands to wash away the dirt, Peter learned lessons that lingered with him to his dying day.

PETER OBSERVED THE HUMILITY OF JESUS

Sudden silence settled over the room as Jesus poured water into the basin from the pitcher, approached a disciple, stooped, then began to wash his feet and wipe them with a towel. Peter watched as Jesus moved to the next disciple, and the next, getting closer and closer.

What love! John commented, "having loved his own which were in the world, he loved them unto the end" (13:1). The Omniscient One, instead of occupying His mind with His imminent betrayal, arrest, trial, and excruciating sufferings, devoted Himself to the needs of His followers.

What humiliation! Though God, He became man. Though the object of heavenly adoration and the Second Person of the Trinity, this Somebody became a nobody. From Master He became servant. Peter may not have grasped the full extent of Jesus's self-abasement at this time, but he did sense enough of it to react to it.

Peter didn't like to see Jesus so meek and lowly. Peter had declared Jesus to be the Christ, the Son of the living God. He had seen Him transfigured with face brighter than the noon-day sun, and his garments flashing like lightning. Only days before he had seen Jesus assertively chase the money-changers out of the temple. To see Him now stoop to washing feet went counter to Jesus' dignity, thought Peter.

So when Jesus finished the feet of the disciple next to him, Peter said, "Lord, dost thou wash my feet?" "Isn't it out of character," he reasoned. Though Peter deserves credit for recognizing the incongruity of the Master washing the disciples' feet, he needed to learn some lessons.

Jesus spoke of Peter's deficiency of understanding, but also promised fuller knowledge later. "What I do thou knowest not now; but thou shalt know hereafter" (vs. 7). If Simon would submit now, he would later discover the significance of the footwashing.

The Lord often delays explanation of His ways. Those suffering under permissive providence in sickness, bereavement, tragedy, or business setback, should take consolation that "some day we'll understand" how trials refine the dross and work for our good.

Peter soon learned what his Master was exemplifying, namely that true greatness consists not in sovereignty, but in service. Scholars think that Mark, long time companion of Peter, though inspired by the Holy Spirit, received much of the material for his Gospel from Peter. If Mark does indeed reflect the thinking of Peter, how significant that he emphasizes the servanthood of Christ, as distinct from Matthew who stresses His kingship, from Luke who depicts His humanity, and from John who portrays His deity.

Mark's Gospel, influenced by Peter, portrays Christ ministering in lowliness and meekness. No genealogy is given, for who cares for the pedigree of a slave? No Sermon on the Mount is found, setting forth the creed of His kingdom, for a servant has no realm. Titles are fewer in Mark— Christ is never mentioned as King save in derision. He is sometimes called "Master" when other Gospels call Him "Lord" (Matthew 8:25; Mark 4:38).

The word translated *immediately, forthwith,* or *straightway,* occurs 40 times in Mark, indicating the urgency and promptness with which a servant should respond to orders.

Twelve of the sixteen chapters begin with "and," conveying action. Mark contains only four parables, but describes numerous miracles. Doesn't a servant talk little but do much? Even the four parables have to do with service (4:3ff., 26ff., 30ff., 12:1ff.).

Both the hand and the eye of the Lord are mentioned frequently (1:31, 5:41; 7:32; 8:22,23,25; 9:27; 3:5,34; 8:33; 10:21; 11:11). Shouldn't a servant use his eye to note what should be done with the hand?

Jesus worked so hard one day that toward evening He fell asleep in a violent storm on Galilee. Only Mark records the events of what A. T. Robertson calls "the busy day," probably typical of dozens of other days in this Servant's life.

Mark closes his Gospel in a striking manner, "The Lord working with them" (16:20).

Christ's example of stooping to a menial task wasn't lost on Peter. Nor should it be missed by us. Late one night during a conference at Moody Bible Institute, D. L. Moody, walking around the halls, came upon guest rooms where visiting English preachers were sleeping. Outside each door was a pair of shoes. Spotting some students, Moody said, "These ministers are following the custom of their country where they always put their shoes out to be cleaned at night. Would you fellows get a piece of chalk from a classroom, put the number of the room on the soles of the shoes, then shine them nicely?"

The students protested, "Mr. Moody, we didn't come to this school to clean shoes. We came here to study for the ministry"—whereupon Moody himself collected the shoes, took them to his room, polished them nicely, and put them back in place.

A man who prided himself on his station in life said with a superior air in a group where the great pioneer-missionary William Carey was present, "I do believe Carey was

once a shoemaker, wasn't he, before he became a missionary?" Overhearing the remark, Carey spoke up, "Oh, no,
I was only a cobbler!" (The archaic meaning of *cobbler* is
clumsy worker.)

PETER LEARNED THE NEED
FOR CLEANSING FROM
DAILY DEFILEMENT

Another reason the Lord washed their feet was to teach
the need of spiritual cleansing. True, their feet had been
made dirty by walking around dusty paths that day. But
their need for cleansing was more than physical. They had
become spiritually defiled.

Recall—the disciples had been arguing like a group
of kids over top spots in the coming kingdom, each asserting,
"I want to be first." How the Lord must have been grieved.
On this night before the crucifixion their hearts should have
been melted in sorrow for their Master, but instead were
filled with pride, greed, and ambition. The Lord's supper
could not be appropriately initiated as long as this mood
of dissension prevailed. Spiritual defilement indeed needed
to be removed. So the Lord started to wash their feet.

But the lesson didn't sink in for a few minutes. At
first, Peter refused Jesus. "Thou shalt never wash my feet."
Though Peter intended this objection to show devotion, it
really displayed disobedience.

Christ came to cleanse us from sin. If Peter refused,
he would be out of tune with the Redeemer's mission. Jesus
replied, "If I wash thee not, thou hast no part with me."

Regeneration must be followed by sanctification.
Christ's purpose is to save us from defilements. If we do
not wish daily cleansing, then we aren't in tune with His
program for us.

Peter recalled the purpose for which Jesus had called

him—to be a fisher of men. He wanted to share in the Master's work, so he rushed to the other extreme, "Lord, not my feet only, but also my hands and my head." One minute he refused permission for Christ to wash one bit of him; now, good old Peter swings to wanting Jesus to wash all of him. This surplus of zeal was as culpable as refusal, for true obedience consists in doing the very thing commanded, neither more nor less. Though true to character in acting impulsively, Peter is to be commended for his willingness to rectify a mistake, even though running to the opposite extreme.

Then Jesus gave some teaching vital to successful Christian living. "He that is washed needeth not save to wash his feet, but is clean every whit: and ye are clean." Two words for *wash* are used in this sentence. The first means to "bathe completely," whereas the second means "partial wash." Someone who had taken a complete bath, wouldn't need another bath on arriving at a friend's house, for just his feet would have become defiled walking the path. Thus he would need only foot-washing. So, the true believer, when overtaken in a fault, doesn't need to become a Christian all over again, but just needs forgiveness for that defilement.

Regeneration is once for all, complete, final. Titus speaks of the "washing of regeneration" (3:5). But every child of God gets defiled in his daily walk, so day-by-day we need to go to Christ for cleansing. Sin doesn't cut the soul off from Christ. The child is still a child in the family even when he disobeys. But the child must confess wrongdoing in order to clear the air and restore fellowship. Handling of sin immediately is a necessary condition for maintaining the fullness of the Spirit.

Jesus added that "not all" were clean, referring to Judas who apparently was never really regenerated.

When their feet were washed (spiritually as well as physically), the disciples were ready for the institution of the Lord's Supper. Their envy, bitterness, pride, and ambition had been washed away. They were in fellowship with their Master and with each other.

But before many hours Peter would need to have his feet washed again because of his denial of Jesus. How comforting this recent lesson would be. He could console himself, "I'm not a castaway. I haven't forfeited my salvation. My name has not been erased from the book of life. I'm still one of the Lord's sheep. But I do need cleansing from my awful defilement." How eagerly he must have poured out his contrition to Jesus during their private resurrection-morning meeting, and thus had his feet washed again.

It's impossible for God's children to walk on the Christian highway without contamination from something we see, hear, say, or think. How wonderful the divine provision, "If we confess our sins, he is faithful and just to forgive us our sins, and to cleanse us from all unrighteousness" (1 John 1:9).

PETER HEARD THE COMMAND TO FOLLOW JESUS' EXAMPLE

Whenever possible, a senior missionary tried to deal with staff problems by personal example instead of by command. When the sewage system backed up one day, creating an awful smell, he found the watchman and the chauffeur arguing over whose responsibility it was to climb down into the slimy hole to clear out the pipe. Each deemed this repulsive task below his dignity. "Since you men are above such lowly labor, I'll do it myself," the missionary told the amazed employees. Then he removed the manhole cover, and despite the nauseating odor, slid down into the sewer. So ashamed were the workmen at their arrogant attitude that the missionary never again had any problem with them over doing menial tasks.

How convicted the apostles must have been at their failure to do the humble assignment, an omission all the more exposed by their Master's act of condescension. His words, when He had completed his round of ablutions, must have hit home with thunderous impact. "If I then, your Lord and Master, have washed your feet; ye also ought to wash one another's feet. For I have given you an example, that ye should do as I have done to you. Verily, verily, I say unto you, The servant is not greater than his lord; neither he that is sent greater than he that sent him. If ye know these things, happy are ye if ye do them" (John 13:14–17).

Some denominations, taking this command literally, practice footwashing as an ordinance, adding it to those of baptism and communion. However, much of Christendom does not understand that our Lord was not commanding a repetition of the act of footwashing, but rather demanding the manifestation of the spirit compelling the Master's act. Not the outward deed, no matter how sincerely done, but the spirit inducing it, is what the Lord seems to have had in mind. None can escape the clear injunction to serve others in need. The insignificant favor of a cup of water given in Jesus' name will not go unrewarded, even when offered to a despised child.

An interesting sidelight in the career of the distinguished apologist and seminary professor of the early part of our century, Dr. J. Gresham Machen, occurred during World War I. Applying for overseas service with the YMCA, he was first assigned the task of making and selling hot chocolate drink in a French village. The process consisted in shaving up large boxes of sweet chocolate, adding a fixed quantity of boiled water, then adding a larger quantity of water, all the time mixing the chocolate in, bringing the whole to a boil, adding condensed milk, and then ending with a final boiling. To open the canteen at 7:00 a.m. meant rising much earlier to prepare the hot drink in time. Though he wished for a different responsibility, especially in Christian service, this ordained and scholarly professor contented himself with the opportunity of performing such menial service.

Meanness of work never lowers a person. Rather the law of spiritual rank says the higher you wish to stand, the lower you must stoop to serve.

The Lord served in ways other than the washing of feet. He broke the loaves and fishes and distributed them to His disciples. He replenished the wine at the Cana wedding. He arranged for the upper room, broke bread, and distributed the cup at the Last Supper. In the Emmaus home after the resurrection He broke bread, though a guest. On the seashore appearance to seven disciples, He prepared the fire and the breakfast, issuing the invitation, "Come and dine." Peter described Him as one "who went about doing good, and healing all that were oppressed of the devil" (Acts 10:38). Though all this time He was Master, He was also Servant, answering the call for help and ministering to the needy.

The example of Christ's service so dominated the early church that the titles given leaders signify service. A minister is simply one who ministers or serves. The word deacon means to minister or serve. A pastor is a servant-shepherd of the flock. A bishop is an overseeing servant. Church leaders are not bosses but servants, as are all believers.

Because Christ stooped in lowly ministry to us, we should stoop to humble deeds for others. He served me, so I should serve my neighbor. His parable of the Good Samaritan teaches that service must be extended to anyone in need that crosses our path, regardless of color or creed.

A brilliant seminary senior and leading orator of his class was called to the pulpit of a large church. Though acclaimed as a coming pulpiteer, the young preacher longed to do more in the spread of the Gospel. Hearing of a mission in a distant city doing a worthy work among the slums, he resigned his church and offered his services. His first assignment was to clean a pile of muddy shoes belonging to his fellow-interns, most of whom had little formal education. As he scraped away the mud, a struggle raged within. Was this why he renounced his fashionable church? He had almost decided to go back to the pastorate when a verse from the Bible came to his mind. "He . . . took a towel, and girded himself." In a moment the victory was won as he cried out, "Lord, if You could take a towel and wash the disciples' dirty feet, surely I can take a brush and clean the interns' dirty boots." Servanthood triumphed, resulting in a sacrificial, yet influential ministry.

The disciples should not have looked the other way from the basin, pitcher and towel that night in the upper room. An excellent motto for lowly service would be, "The basin stops here."

Was the picture of Jesus wrapping the towel around His waist on that eventful night so vivid in Peter's memory the reason he later wrote, "Yea, all of you be subject one to another, and be clothed with humility: for God resisteth the proud, but giveth grace to the humble" (1 Peter:5).

8

The Denial

(Matthew 26:31–35,58,69–75; Mark 14:27–
31,54,66–72; Luke 22:31–34,54–62; John
18:15–18,25–27)

When technology suffered a series of setbacks in the late '70s, one cartoonist combined several in one disaster. His cartoon showed Skylab falling on a DC-10 cargo plane. The DC-10 was loaded with Pintos, each equipped with Firestone 500 tires. It all crashed on Three Mile Island, Pennsylvania, where the residents put out the fire with hair dryers lined with asbestos.

The denial of his Master was indeed the culmination of a day of disaster in Simon Peter's life. Earlier he argued with other disciples over who would be greatest in the kingdom. Then he at first refused to let Jesus wash his feet. More than once he boasted he would die for Jesus, if necessary. In Gethsemane he fell asleep when he should have been watching. When the mob came to arrest Jesus, he chopped off the ear of the high priest's servant. Finally, in the courtyard he blatantly and blasphemously denied he ever knew Jesus.

Note that his position as leader of the Twelve did not exempt Peter from temptation. Rather, it probably made him top target for Satan's darts.

WHY PETER DENIED THE LORD

A kidnapper abducted an eight-year-old girl in the morning, drove around with her, phoned for a ransom, then

96

without trying to collect the money, let her out near her home unharmed. When he was caught, his fellow-citizens were amazed, for he had been a model citizen. But no person falls suddenly. Nor did Peter. Certain elements made for internal weakness which preceded his exterior fall.

His Over Self-confidence

Despite strong warnings, Peter fell. Through His divine foresight Jesus knew all the disciples would flee. He told them, "All ye shall be offended because of me this night." To this Peter replied, "Although all shall be offended, yet will not I." Then Jesus spoke specifically to Peter, "Verily I say unto thee, That this day, even in this night, before the cock crow twice, thou shalt deny me thrice." This only elicited a more vehement reaction from Peter, "If I should die with thee, I will not deny thee in any wise" (Mark 14:27–31). Though all the disciples said the same, Peter was the most dogmatic.

Luke adds that Jesus told Peter, "Simon, Simon, behold, Satan hath desired to have you, that he may sift you as wheat: But I have prayed for thee, that thy faith fail not" (22:31,32). Again the same response from Peter, "I am ready to go with thee, both into prison, and to death" (22:33).

Loud protestation often precedes low performance. The biggest braggadocio in the camp may turn out to be the biggest coward in the conflict. The best swimmer may be in great danger of drowning. The unsinkable Titanic sank. Overconfidence tends to carelessness. The Master knew Peter perfectly. Simon was ignorant of his weakness. Had a fellow-disciple recounted to Peter a few weeks in advance the horrendous details of his denial, Peter might have asked, "Am I a dog that I would do that?"

As the battle ebbed and flowed over the field at Waterloo, Napoleon, stronger in guns, material and men, actually sent three messages to Paris, stating he had won the victory. Many supposedly strong Christians of ten years ago never dreamed then that today, a decade later, they would rarely darken the door of a church, scarcely open their Bibles, attend church, or be involved in any Christian service. The Bible warns, "Wherefore let him that thinketh he standeth take heed lest he fall" (1 Corinthians 10:12).

Says the poet, William Cowper,

> *"Beware of Peter's word,*
> *Nor confidently say,*
> *'I never will deny Thee, Lord',*
> *But, 'Grant I never may'."*

Says Pilgrim's Progress,

> *"He that is down, need fear no fall;*
> *He that is low, no pride.*
> *He that is humble ever shall*
> *Have God to be his guide."*

Failure to Watch and Pray

After the supper in the Upper Room, the apostolic band crossed the brook Kedron into the Garden of Gethsemane. Leaving eight of the disciples, Jesus took the inner three--Peter, James, and John—and asked them to watch and pray. A stone's throw away, the Lord "offered up prayers and supplications with strong crying and tears" (Hebrews 5:7). How He needed the sympathy and proximity of the disciples. But though they could likely hear his half-sobs and anguish, their eyes were heavy with slumber. While their Master agonized midst the gnarled and knotted olive trees, they fell asleep.

After such a warning about his denial, Peter should have zealously thrown himself in supplication for divine help, but spiritual negligence heaped upon his over self-confidence. So, he slumbered physically and spiritually. When the Master returned, He chided them, singling Peter out by name, "Simon, sleepest thou? couldest thou not watch one hour?" (Mark 14:37). In effect, "You who affirmed your love so loudly, could you not keep alert for one hour?"

When Jesus returned to His spot to pray some more, back to sleep went Simon and the others. A second time He found them sleeping. Embarrassed, they did not know how to answer Him (Mark 14:40). The third time He awakened them as the soldiers were approaching to seize Him.

The strong desire of early Puritans to learn from their pastors led them to hire a tithingman to keep them awake during Sunday sermons. As the pastor went to his "tenthly" or "twenty-fifthly" point, even the most zealous Puritans had been known to doze or nod off, especially when drugged by hazy summer days or soothed by the sound of crickets. The moment a parishioner dropped off to sleep, or even "rested his eyes," the tithingman would reach out his staff and poke the sleepyhead, usually with a foxtail on one end for the ladies, or a brass knob for men.

One tithingman in Massachusetts had a sharp thorn on the end of his staff for sound sleepers. On the first Sunday in June 1646, on spying a certain gentleman sleeping in the corner with his head against the wall, he thrust the staff to give him a vigorous prick on the hand. The gentleman, quite drowsy, jumped to his feet and exclaimed profanely, "Curse ye, woodchuck!", dreaming some animal had bit his hand. Realizing what had happened, he was much embarrassed, and did not fall asleep soon again in a service.

But spiritual sleepiness has more serious consequences. Failure to watch and pray can lead to the neglect of the Word, absence from church, disobedience of divine commandments, making us easier prey for major temptation.

Peter should have cast himself on the Lord for strength.

No wonder he wrote later, "be ye therefore sober, and watch unto prayer" (1 Peter 4:7).

Fighting When He Should Have Been Submitting

Suddenly, like giant fireflies, in the distance flashed the torches of an approaching mob. Judas was leading a cohort of soldiers, probably a couple hundred of men, joined by a motley crowd of ruffians, armed with swords and clubs. They descended on the garden and headed toward Jesus.

Amazed that his Master let himself be captured, Peter, in a hopeless gesture, reached for his sword, concealed under his cloak and lashed out in blind fury, swinging at the man nearest him, intending to make two out of him. Instead, he severed the right ear of Malchus, a servant of the high priest. Jesus rebuked Peter, telling him to put up his sword. Then He healed the servant's ear. Peter ran.

By fighting, Peter was out of tune with the Master's kingdom. Christ came to suffer and die on the cross. If the Master's kingdom were to come by force, then his servants would have fought. Fighting might have ended the Savior's life by sword or by club. Then the cross would have been thwarted and Christ's voluntary sacrifice prevented.

Peter showed physical bravery in his willingness to defend Jesus. But his physical courage sadly contrasted to his subsequent moral cowardice. Some find it easy to play heroic football when the fans are cheering, but hard to be honest on the final exam when no one is watching.

Failure to appreciate the cross and to use its provisions for victory over temptation leaves us vulnerable to backsliding in our Christian life. We need to pray, "Jesus, Keep Me Near the Cross."

He Followed Afar Off

Moments later as the murmur of voices faded and flickering torches disappeared across the brook, Peter realized that Jesus was on His way to trial, and possible death. He couldn't understand the calm surrender of Jesus, like a lamb led to the slaughter. Stumbling back to the path, the branches of his hiding-place stinging his face, he hurried to catch the procession. But he kept his distance, not anxious to get too close after wounding the high priest's servant. His own arrest, or some retaliation at least, was possible.

A little while later, Peter wandered into the high priest's courtyard to warm himself at the fire. Sadly, he became one of the crowd, not distinct from it. He was in the world, and of it. To enter an atheist's house is all right, but all wrong to espouse his cause. Perhaps Peter should have gone and stood beside Jesus. At least he should have stood up for Him in that crowd. But over self-confidence, failure to watch and pray, fighting instead of submitting, and following afar off, led to denial.

THE DENIAL ITSELF

The four accounts of the denial are difficult to reconcile. One problem is the crowing of the cock. Mark says the bird crowed twice, while the other Gospels simply state that before the cock would crow Peter would deny the Lord three times.

No contradiction exists. The other Gospels did not affirm that the cock crowed *only* once as opposed to Mark's twice. They simply referred to the cock-crowing without specifying once or twice. "Cockcrowing" was a colloquial expression for early morning, also designated the third of four Roman night watches. Thus three Gospels presented the main point of Jesus' warning that Peter would deny the Lord three times before early morning which was signalled by the cockcrowing. But Mark recounted the added detail of a second cockcrowing.

More difficult to harmonize are the three denials themselves. Because the denials seem to number more than three, some have suggested that the denials totaled six, three before each cockcrowing. However, a more plausible explanation seems to call for three periods of denial rather than three specific denials by three separate persons. In fact, in the second and third denials Peter seems to be assailed on each occasion by one or more individuals, and then by a group.

Peter's denials become successively more intense. The first was a simple denial. The second was accompanied by an oath (Matthew 26:72). The third was vehemently followed by cursing (26:74).

First Denial—At the Door

As the crowd of soldiers headed for the house of high-priest Annas, Peter followed from a distance. To gain access to the courtyard meant passing through a gate. But a maid was scrutinizing those wishing to enter. How would he gain admittance? To his surprise he found a friend there, probably John, whose influence brought Peter in.

But the maid-gatekeeper, looking closely at Peter, exclaimed, "Art not thou also one of this man's disciples?" Immediately he retorted, "I am not" (John 18:17).

Peter, we stand amazed! Weren't you in the company of Jesus for three years. Haven't you just taken the Lord's Supper? Don't you remember the day when at His command you cast your net down and caught so many fish the net broke? Has the shock of all this dulled your memory?

Second Denial—By the Fire

Because the night was frosty, the servants built a fire in the open quadrangle. As Peter huddled near the warmth, he pulsated inwardly with sympathy for Christ, but he wanted those around him to believe him indifferent to the prisoner. So as the conversation ranged from coarse jokes to latest tidbits of life at Rome, he did his best to blend into the scenery.

Suddenly he was jolted to reality by a maid, who glimpsing his face from the reflection of the fire, exclaimed, "Thou also wast with Jesus of Galilee" (Matthew 26:69). Peter denied the accusation before them all.

Then when he went out into the porch, another maid recognized him, "This man also was with Jesus of Nazareth" (26:71). Peter denied with an oath, calling God in heaven to witness to his statement. It was as though Peter said, "I promise to tell the truth, the whole truth, and everything but the truth."

About this time, another (masculine) saw him and said, "Thou also art one of them. But Peter said, Man, I am not" (Luke 22:58).

Another gospel records that while Peter was around the fire, they said to him, "Art thou also one of his disciples?" The "they" could refer to the maids and the man, or to servants and soldiers standing around the fire, or to all collectively.

Peter, wait a minute! Remember how you saw Him restore sight to blind Bartimaeus. Recall the lame man at the pool of Bethesda. How could you forget the raising of Lazarus?

Third Denial—An Hour Later

An hour passed. To cover his nervousness Peter joined in the chatter periodically. But his accent gave him away. A relative of the servant whose ear had been severed pointed to Peter, "Did not I see thee in the garden with him?" (John 18:26). This relative may be the same person referred to in Luke 22:59.

The two other gospels speak of a group confronting Peter. "They that stood by" accused him, "Of a truth thou also art one of them; for thy speech betrayeth thee" (Matthew 26:73; Mark 14:70). In no mood to be badgered by a bunch of unfeeling servants and soldiers who thought it a good joke to torment him by working on his fears, Peter began to curse and swear. In the garden he had let loose with his sword. Now he lets loose with his tongue, swearing not like a trooper, but like a Galilean fisherman.

No wonder that a few moments later, after the cock crowed a second time and Jesus looked in his direction, that Peter went out and wept bitterly.

WE CAN DENY CHRIST IN MANY WAYS

John Knox, bold Scottish preacher, approached the court of Bloody Mary, an avowed enemy of the preacher. He was advised to postpone his visit as she was in an angry mood. He kept right on walking toward her throne, remarking, "Why should I be afraid of a queen when I have just spent four hours with God?" The fear of man brings a snare. Peter found this out, as he cowed in the midst of his Master's enemies. Fear of ridicule may lead us to deny Christ in a variety of ways.

By Silence

Failure to speak up for Jesus when we should is tacit denial. A proverb says, "Silence is golden; sometimes it's yellow." A man who became a Christian went off to work in a lumber camp. When he returned, his pastor asked if he suffered much ridicule because he was a Christian. "Not a bit," the lumberjack replied, "because they never found out."

By Inconsistency

The professing believer who tells a lie denies the God of truth. The Christian who gets involved in immorality denies the God of purity. The church member who cheats on his income tax or in business denies the God of honesty. Paul wrote about those who profess to know God, but who deny Him in works (Titus 1:16). What we are speaks so loudly that people often cannot hear what we say.

By Un-Christlike Attitude

Bitter reaction to trouble denies our faith in the goodness of God. Patient acceptance is a good advertisement for the Christian witness.

A church in New York state suffered a summer of tragedies. One officer died suddenly of a heart attack. The wife of another board member died of cancer. Then one night the chairman of the board was killed in an automobile accident. Several members gathered informally in the pastor's home the evening of the tragedy, weeping, yet rejoicing through the comfort of Christ. In the parsonage was an 89-year-old man, whom the pastor and wife had taken in for several weeks till a room in a nursing home became

available. He was an agnostic who was quite willing to up-
hold his views in conversations with the pastor. The night
of the accident was the old man's final night there; the next
morning he was to move into the nursing home. After all
had left he said to the pastor, "I have to make a decision."
The pastor thought it had to do with his move to a new
location. The old man continued, "I need to make a decision
to accept Christ as my Savior. I've watched your members
all summer, and especially tonight. I've seen their strength
in the midst of tragedy!"

In whatever way may be open to us, we need to confess
Christ before men. In the Middle Ages the governor of the
north African city of Algiers, learning that a captive had
designed many of Europe's largest buildings, called him to
the palace. "We want you to build a very beautiful mosque.
You are to be in charge of designing it."

If he refused, the Christian knew they might execute
him. Though he was willing to die for his faith, he first
wished to make a real testimony to these Moslems who
didn't know the message of the cross. A bold plan popped
into his mind and he accepted the assignment and with the
advice of the governor selected lovely slabs of marble, some
of which had to be shipped hundreds of miles.

Months later came the day the building was finished.
The Christian's pulse pounded faster when anyone looked
at the building, lest they discover his secret. The marble
dazzled in the afternoon sun. As the governor assembled
his people, he mused, "How funny! We forced a Christian
architect to build a Moslem temple. This will show Christians in Europe how powerful we Moslems are."

The governor ordered the slave to step forward to the
marble steps of the new building. "You have built the most
beautiful mosque I have ever seen—a great reminder of the
Moslem faith."

"That's not true, your honor," the Christian said quickly. The crowd grew silent, amazed that the Christian dare talk back to their governor.

"Isn't this a place for Moslems to worship Mohammed?" the governor flushed with anger.

"Yes," said the believer. "They can worship Mohammed, if they want to. It's your building now. But it has been built in such a way as to always remind people that Jesus Christ is the only hope of heaven. I love Jesus with all my heart."

"What do you mean?" the governor roared.

"One thing you haven't noticed," replied the Christian. But once I tell my secret, it will always remind your country of Jesus, Who shed His blood on a cross so we could be forgiven." Then quietly the Christian slave pointed to the four directions inside the great mosque. "See, I have built the mosque in the shape of a cross. May it ever remind you of my Lord and Savior Jesus Christ?"

According to a chaplain who served in that area in World War II, the Christian was put to death immediately, but the mosque still stands, the cross visible to visitors to Algiers today as a confession of this Christian captive's unashamed faith in Christ.

An old man left his farm to visit his son, a congressman in Washington. The congressman introduced his old father to an ambassador from an eastern nation. The father, a zealous Christian, almost immediately asked the ambassador if he were a Christian. Before an answer could come, the much-embarrassed son interrupted, and whisked his father away. Soon after, the old man caught pneumonia and passed away. Among the flowers at the funeral were roses from the ambassador. A note brought tears to the congressman's eyes, "Your father is the only man in America who ever asked me if I were a Christian!"

Jesus said, "Whosoever therefore shall confess me before men, him will I confess also before my Father which is in heaven. But whosoever shall deny me before men, him will I also deny before my Father which is in heaven" (Matthew 10:32,33).

A New Lease on Life

(John 21:1–19)

When the summer-long Billy Graham crusade was held in New York's Madison Square Garden in 1957, the campaign included a late nightly TV program, *Impact,* emceed by Mel Dibble, a folksy, experienced performer, thoroughly at home in the television medium. His face and voice at the start and finish of the Saturday night nation-wide telecasts from the Garden made him familiar to millions across the land.

What most people didn't know was that Mel Dibble had been away from the Lord for several years. In earlier years he had attended Moody Bible Institute and Wheaton College, had been assistant pastor at a large Michigan Baptist church, regular soloist at Philadelphia's Tenth Presbyterian Church, and also song-leader each summer at Percy Crawford's Pinebrook Camp. Then he entered the entertainment world, for four years emceeing mid-western TV network breakfast programs. During those years he seldom attended church, neglected Bible and prayer, and tottered on the verge of alcoholism and marriage breakup. He needed to turn back to the Lord.

Four years before the New York crusade, through the influence of Billy Graham and Dr. Donald Gray Barnhouse, he came back to the Lord. He literally walked away from his TV career, and has been active in evangelism from that day.

Peter, after his unbelievable defection from his Master, needed to be restored. Things were dark. But Jesus had said, "Satan hath desired to have you, that he may sift you as wheat; But I have prayed for thee, that thy faith fail not" (Luke 22:31,32).

At the very moment of Peter's final denial, soldiers were leading Jesus away. Peter's strident voice carried through the courtyard, echoing its curses. As the vehement flow of oaths dwindled to silence, the cock crowed the second time. Something struck home to Peter's conscience. He recalled the Master's prophecy. At that second Jesus turned and looked at Peter. What a look! Jesus had heard every blistering denial, every false oath, every blasphemous curse. Their eyes met for one unforgettable moment. Then hot tears flooded Peter's eyes, blurring vision. He turned and rushed into the night, weeping bitterly.

Peter slept little that night. The next day—the day of the cross—he wept again and again. And again through the Sabbath. Guilt burned in his soul—falsehood, evasion, ingratitude, cowardice, profanity—aggravated by his great privilege of three years in the company as leader among the disciples, after solemn warnings by Jesus, and in the hour of his Master's greatest need. This once eager and devoted apostle cringed like a whipped dog, life crushed from him, nursing shame, almost beside himself with despair. How he needed a new lease on life! And he was to get it.

THE WORD OF ENCOURAGEMENT

Early that first Easter came the initial word from the Lord that cheered Peter's fallen spirit. An angel at the tomb had given the women this message, "He is risen ... tell his disciples and Peter" (Mark 16:6,7).

The added words, "and Peter" are found only in Mark whose Gospel bears strong traces of Peter's influence. Peter could never forget that the angel singled him out, doubtless at the command of Jesus. This special attention for Peter removed some of his anguish, giving him comfort and hope after those wretched hours. His Master still cared for him! Mercy was replacing misery. Perhaps, after all, he could be forgiven for his infamy. Says the poetess,

> *"How like our Lord to add, 'and Peter'—knowing*
> *That one would walk the world in cruel shame,*
> *Forever haunted by a far cock crowing,*
> *An idle boast, and eyes that held no blame*
> *But looked with grave compassionate reminding*
> *Into his own. How like our Lord, to know*
> *That somewhere Peter, stumbling through*
> *   blinding*
> *And bitter tears, would need that message so."*

> *"That somewhere Peter, all his spirit broken,*
> *Past pride, past fear, past all save grim regret,*
> *Would find in two small words a tender token*
> *That all his lifetime he would not forget:*
> *The sweet assurance that he still belonged,*
> *In spite of all, unto the Lord he wronged."*
>
> —Helen Frazee-Bower, title of poem,
> "And Peter" in "He Came
> with Music," Moody Press,
> Chicago, 1963, p. 42

As soon as Mary Magdalene brought the word, Peter and John hurried to the sepulcher. One tradition suggests that on the night of his bitter weeping Peter had been found by John who took the broken-hearted Peter home with him. Whether they were staying at the same address, or lodging in separate homes, we do not know. But we are sure that

John did outrun Peter to the grave, perhaps because he was younger, but also likely because Peter's debilitated condition, due to weeping and sleepiness, made his legs lumber heavily along.

Though John outran Peter to the grave, it was Peter who entered first. Peter walked right past John, who was hesitating at the door. Inside he saw the linen clothes and headpiece lying separately. Since our Lord was recognized less by His appearance than by His mannerisms, such as the tone of voice to Mary, the breaking of bread in Emmaus, and the miracle on Galilee, perhaps Peter recognized Jesus' particular manner of folding His clothes. At any rate, John joined Peter within. Faith came alive.

THE PRIVATE INTERVIEW

Sometime before evening on that first Easter, Christ confronted Peter. Wistfully, we wonder where and when. In this private interview Peter blurted out in full confession all the shame of his several denials.

We imagine Jesus answering like this. "Simon, remember how I told you I must die, and rise the third day. You were so upset about the cross that you never understood about the rising. Simon, recall how I warned you that you would deny Me. But I told you I would pray for you that your faith fail not. It hasn't failed. Simon, I went to the cross for all your sins. Now I'm the living Lord. Your denials are forgiven. Grieve no more!"

Simon couldn't keep the joy of this appearance to himself. Soon the word circulated among the disciples, "The Lord is risen indeed, and hath appeared to Simon" (Luke 24:34). In the great Corinthian resurrection chapter, this appearance to Peter tops the list of those to whom the risen Christ appeared (1 Corinthians 15:5).

Backsliding

Peter wasn't the last backslider. Jerry McAuley, a river-thief operating in New York City, was converted in Sing Sing prison. For a while he rejoiced in his salvation, began to witness to fellow-prisoners, urged many to read their Bibles, and led many to conversion.

After serving half his sentence, he received a pardon from the governor. On release he became more lonely than when in his cell, for he couldn't go back to his old haunts and pals. He lamented, "If I'd only had one single Christian friend at that time, it would have saved me years of misery."

Before long he yielded to temptation to take a drink. Then began a sad tale of backsliding. For four years he led a desperate, reckless life in which he became a gambler, prize-fighter, ruffian, drunkard, and river-thief. Many were his narrow escapes from death on the waterfront.

Then a home missionary doing door-to-door visitation struck up a friendship with McAuley. Through persistent personal work and concern so deep he would have given the coat off his back to keep McAuley from going out on the river at night to steal, this missionary led him back to Christ. A vision of rescue mission work in his old district led to the start of the McAuley Water Street Mission.

A backslider's diary read thus:

January: I hereby resolve to start to attend church this year, but I'll wait till February. I have to get over the holiday.

February: Weather terrible. I'll wait till it warms up a bit.

March: Lots of sickness now. Must keep away from those bugs.

April: Easter. Big crowds. They won't miss me.

May:	I've been holed up all winter. Now that the weather is better it's time to hold reunions, and get away weekends.
June:	I'll wait till the baby is older. How on earth do some folks bring their babies at two weeks of age . . . and then never miss a Sunday at worship?
July:	Boy, the heat is terrific! That air conditioning in the church might give me the chills. Anyhow we've got that cabin and boat for Sundays.
August:	Preacher's on vacation. He'll never know if I miss. Never liked those guest preachers anyhow, but when preacher gets back . . .
Sept:	School's started. Vacation threw me behind in my work. Got to make one last visit to my relatives before the snow flies.
October:	Leaves are beautiful this time of year. I can worship God outdoors anyhow. Will be cooped up all winter . . . so . . .
November:	Getting colder . . . can't stand warm church buildings with a lot of people crowding me.
December:	This is the month of Christmas. It belongs to the kids. I don't have time now for the church. Besides the roads are so bad. Anyway, next month is January and I'll resolve to get started first thing next year."

Backsliders can be restored. The Lord longs to have them back in fellowship with Himself. Christ had prayed for Peter. He had also given him such a look that he went out and wept bitterly. Now he had privately rehabilitated him. But because the denial had been public, the Master arranged a public restoration and recommissioning.

THE PUBLIC AFFIRMATION

John 21, with its account of Peter's public reinstatement, really comprises an appendage to the fourth Gospel. Written to show the deity of Christ, the book reaches its climax in Thomas' confession, "My Lord and my God" (20:28). Then comes the digressive epilogue with its lovely story of Peter's restoration. If this incident had been omitted, we might have puzzled at Peter's leadership in the upper room, his preaching at Pentecost, and his prominence in the early chapters of Acts, since our last full view would have portrayed him a blaspheming, Christ-denying failure. After his discrediting experience, the story in John 21 accredits Peter to the New Testament reader. Since the veil of silence was so tightly drawn over the private meeting of Jesus and Peter, the epilogue vindicates the elevation, in less than two months, of the Peter of denials to the Peter of Pentecost.

Back in Galilee soon after the resurrection, Peter, ever the leader, said, "I go a fishing" (21:3). Going fishing did not mean that he was giving up his discipleship and going back to his old trade. The Master had told them to go into Galilee where they would see Him again (Matthew 28:10). But since they did not know how long it would be before He would appear, Peter proposed temporary resumption of their former craft till new orders came from their risen Lord.

On their overnight fishing expedition something happened to remind them of a similar incident two years before. Again, after a night of fruitless toil, the Master directed them to an immense catch, showing them anew that without Him their usual occupation was fruitless. In this graphically repeated episode He wanted them to understand that their livelihood would be obtained, not by their fishing, but from food His hand would provide and by fires He would light.

The Lord didn't reprimand Peter for fishing, but did remind him that he had other business to do.

After they hauled in their miraculous haul of 153 fish, they were invited by Jesus to "come and dine." With the meal over, He broached the unfinished business. Since Peter had publicly denied the Lord, now he must be publicly restored. Though he had been reconciled in a private talk with Jesus, perhaps the apostolic band had some doubt about Peter's fervor after such vehement denials. So the Lord asked for a decisive expression of Peter's loyalty.

The scene set by the Master exhibited several similarities to the denial scene. The denials were made not long after eating, mostly around or near a fire, and were three in number. Now they had just dined, were sitting around a fire, and three affirmations were given.

A king gave all his major officers a new name suggested by their outstanding quality. When any displeased him, he reverted to his old name, which then caused alarm. Perhaps the Lord's use of Peter's old name in his question, "Simon, lovest thou me more than these?" was designed to remind him of the treachery of his old nature. "More than these" likely referred, not to the fish which represented his former business interests, but to the apostles whose devotion Peter had implied was inferior to his (Matthew 26:33).

The old Simon would have boasted of his love. Now no protestation of superior love escaped his lips. Rather, he used a milder word to pledge his love than the word Jesus employed. Jesus used the word which expresses the highest form of unconditional love, whereas Peter replied with a term which stands for affection.

A second time Jesus asked Peter if he loved Him, using the same higher term. A second time Peter answered, utilizing the same less intense word for affection. Then the third time the Lord descended to Peter's more moderate word. Peter, grieved because the question was asked three times, gushed out, "Lord, you know everything. You know that I have genuine affection for you," using the same word for love he had employed the first two times.

Peter's self-judgement was complete. His restoration did not require a rehashing of previous sin. His excessive self-confidence has been tripped up sufficiently to make him see his helplessness apart from Christ. The boastful man, humbled by his weakness, was now qualified to strengthen his brethren. Three times he was so commissioned. "Feed my lambs. Tend my sheep. Feed my sheep." An old Syriac version refers to the tending and feeding of lambs, ewes, and sheep.

But the Lord was not finished. He took Peter back to his grandiose affirmation, "I will go with thee to prison and to death." To which He said, in effect, "Peter, you shall have this honor also. Verily, verily I say unto thee, when thou wast young thou girdest thyself, and walkedst whither thou wouldest; but when thou shalt be old, thou shalt stretch forth thy hands, and another shall gird thee, and carry thee whither thou wouldest not. This spake he, signifying by what death he should glorify God. And when he had spoken this he said unto him, Follow me" (John 21:18,19).

Peter's love would be put to the test, for he would die by crucifixion. This time, with realistic self-appraisal, he faced the fact that to serve and follow his Master would involve losing his life in an excruciating manner.

An artist visited his little granddaughter. On arrival he found her standing in a corner with her face to the wall as punishment for misbehavior. A tactful grandfather, he did not interfere with the discipline. But a few minutes later he took out his paints, went to the corner where the little girl had to stand, and there painted pictures on the wall for her amusement. When Peter was put in the corner for his denial, his experience provided a backdrop for the restoring mercy of Christ. Where sin abounded, grace did much more abound.

In some free verse titled *Judas*, Peter says,

because we are all
betrayers, guilty, taking
silver and eating
body and blood and asking
is it I and hearing him
say yes
it would be easy for us all
to rush out
and hang ourselves
but if we find grace
to cry and wait out the days
after the voice
of morning has crowed
in our ears and broken
our hearts
he will be there
to ask us each again
do you love me"

—Luci Shaw in *Christianity Today*, 6 April 79, p. 17.

A Latin hymn alleges that Peter never heard a cock crow without falling to his knees to weep. Another tradition claims it became his custom to wake daily at cock-crow to spend an hour in prayer, the fatal hour in which he had failed his Lord. These extra-canonical stories suggest that Peter's life was stronger because of his fall. Indeed he became a new man.

"O Hope of every contrite heart,
O Joy of all the meek,
To those who fall, how kind Thou art!
How good to those who seek!"

—Bernard of Clairvaux

A soldier, the picture of misery, stumbled into the army chaplain's office, mumbling, "I've hauled down the flag, sir!" The soldier was the chaplain's right-hand assistant who constantly invited servicemen to the chapel, was a strong influence for good in the barracks, and often sang a gospel solo. "I was out with the men last night, and they got me to drink. They had to carry me back to my quarters. I'm ashamed of myself. I've hauled down the flag!"

Trying to hide his disappointment, the chaplain countered, "Even if you've hauled down the flag, you know enough about the mercy of Christ and of His power to haul the flag up again."

"Yes, sir, I've confessed to God. I know He has forgiven me. But how can I ever face the boys again?"

The chaplain stood to his feet. "We're going to kneel down right here, both of us, and consecrate ourselves anew to God. Tonight we'll have the regular service and I want you to sing a solo. It will be hard, but don't fail to turn up."

That night when his name was announced to sing, everyone gasped. Some smirked, "What an old hypocrite!" The soldier began, "Listen, you know all about me, and the chaplain knows too. I hauled down the flag last night, but by God's grace I've hauled it up again." Then he told how he had confessed his sin to God, and how the wonderful love of Christ welcomed him back. He concluded, "Will you let me sing to you again?" Muffled murmurs gave assent. The soldier sang,

> *"When I fear my faith will fail*
> *Christ will hold me fast;*
> *When the tempter would prevail,*
> *He can hold me fast."*

The next day one of the soldiers asked to speak with the chaplain. "I was one of the men who tempted your soloist to drink the other night. We thought it was a joke. But I tell you, when I heard him sing last night, I called on God to forgive me. From now on I'm going to live for Him!"

Every backslider may take hope in the restoration of Peter. With the poet he may say,

"Jesus, let Thy pitying eye
Call back a wandering sheep;
False to Thee, like Peter, I
Would fain, like Peter, weep.

"Let me be by grace restored;
On me be all long-suffering shown;
Turn and look upon me, Lord,
And melt my heart of stone."

in William M. Taylor, *Peter,* London,
Charles Burnet & Co., 1888, p. 333

The Lord does not cast us out. Rather, He puts a new song in our mouth, and teaches us to exclaim, "He restoreth my soul; he leadeth me in the paths of righteousness for his name's sake." He gladly heals our backsliding, for He loves us fully and freely.

10

The New Peter

(Acts 1,2)

A dwarf, standing up, will find himself taller than a giant lying down.

Many Christians compare themselves to Peter in the days of his failures. "I'm so like Peter," they say, "I deny my Lord, too." Thus consoling themselves in their backsliding, not-too-strong believers feed their spiritual self-satisfaction by lording it over Peter, flat because of his shortcomings.

But we should compare ourselves, not with Peter *down*, but with Peter *up*, as he moves boldly through the pages of Acts and provides us with a more positive model to follow.

The Peter of Acts seems so unlike the Peter of the Gospels. Cowardice has given way to courage. Previously frightened by a single maid, he now stands tall before thousands of people and then before the Sanhedrin, without a tremor. Before, he had been a mixture of good impulses and major mistakes. Now he is sober-minded and a tower of strength for his brethren. Clay has been transformed into rock.

THE ACCEPTED LEADER

As the book of Acts opens, Peter is the undisputed leader. In fact, he seems to take the place of Christ in center stage. But in reality Christ is still very much the Head of the Church, though invisibly at work.

A teacher asked his Sunday school class the title of the fifth book of the New Testament. When the universal response was "Acts" or "Acts of the Apostles," the teacher insisted the correct answer was, "The Acts of the Risen Christ through the Apostles." The teacher based his statement on the first two verses of Acts which imply a two-phase ministry of Christ. Whereas the Gospels record "all that Jesus began both to do and teach unto the day in which he was taken up"—His earthly ministry, Acts chronicles all He does after His ascension—His heavenly ministry. In the Gospels Christ was physically present, working with His disciples. In Acts He is in heaven, bodily absent, but nevertheless working through them. Though Peter becomes the leading personality of the first half of Acts, it is still the Person of Christ working by His Holy Spirit empowering the apostles.

Peter Led the Devotional Exercises

Four groups are listed as present in the upper room in the ten days between the Ascension and Pentecost: the eleven disciples by name, the women, the family of Jesus, and other followers which made a total of 120. But standing first of all in the listing of the groups is the name of Peter (Acts 1:13–15).

The main occupation of the 120 during this period was prayer. Peter doubtless set the tone of devotion. Likely, the 120 represented all of the believers in Jerusalem at this time. Though believers need to pray privately each day, they also need to come together collectively at regular intervals for corporate supplications. John Wesley said, "There is no such thing as solitary religion."

Since only 12 of the 120 were named, 90 percent are unnamed, many of them women. Many of God's prayer troops are unsung and unknown, never climb a church platform, or never have their name printed in a church bulletin or denominational paper, but will receive heavenly approval in the day of rewards, as many that are last shall be first.

For what did they pray? Probably not for the coming of the Spirit; that was a foregone conclusion. The apostles had been charged to wait in Jerusalem for the gift of the Spirit. The promise was unconditional. The verb was not subjunctive, "You *might* be baptized with the Holy Ghost not many days hence," but rather simple future, "Ye *shall* be baptized." The *might* would have caused soul-searching in the company of the 120, but no demand was placed on the group, nor conditions laid down. The Spirit was not to be a reward for effort or faith on the part of the recipient, but a gift not to be obtained as a result of human effort.

Peter probably led them in praying for the impact of the coming Spirit's power through their witness on the thousands of unbelievers in Jerusalem. They would need divine unction for any preaching in that religious capital, site of their Master's trial and crucifixion. As a result of their praying, their Holy Ghost boldness led to the conversion of 3,000 in one day, and up to 5,000 a few weeks later.

Today believers need to pray for the blessed Holy Spirit to empower the various ministries of our church life.

Peter Led the Business Session

Peter's leadership was again exercised in the choice of a successor for the betrayer. Showing from the Old Testament that Judas' "bishopric" needed replacing, Peter stated the qualification for apostleship required association with Christ in His earthly ministry from the Baptism of John to the Resurrection, of which he must be a witness. Two names were appointed. Prayer was offered. Lots were cast. Matthias was chosen and numbered with the apostles (Acts 1:15–26). Incidentally, the lot is never again mentioned as a method of divine guidance. With the coming of the Holy Spirit in the next chapter, believers would turn to Him for counsel.

Some think Peter acted like his old self, impulsively, in the choice of a successor for Judas. Had Peter waited, it is claimed, the Lord would have revealed Paul as the choice.

However, the New Testament seems to sanction the validity of Matthias' appointment. His choice was never questioned by the apostles or the church. Matthias, though not mentioned by name, evidently acted with the other eleven (Acts 2:4; 6:2; 9:27; 1 Corinthians 15:5,7).

Though Paul repeatedly asserted His apostleship, he never claimed inclusion with the Twelve. In fact, he did not qualify for apostleship in the restricted sense, for he did not accompany Christ on any of His earthly ministry, much less from the baptism of John. He recognized the Twelve as separate from himself (1 Corinthians 15:5,7). When he met the apostles in Jerusalem, he gave no hint that he considered himself among the Twelve (Galatians 2:1–10).

Rather than acting prematurely, Peter seems to have moved responsibly, even "of necessity" as a fulfillment of Old Testament prophecies (Acts 1:16,22). Note too that Peter did not dictate the choice unilaterally, but let the 120 democratically select two nominees, then cast their lots to make the decision.

Peter's leadership was not only asserted during the ten-day pre-Pentecost period, but all through the early chapters of Acts. Not till Acts 15 do we find this leadership apparently relinquished to James, brother of Jesus, who rendered the verdict at the first Jerusalem council (vs. 13).

THE BOLD WITNESS

Not only did Peter become an accepted and mature leader, but he became an emboldened preacher, as recorded in one of the most triumphant chapters of Scripture. Through his Spirit-empowered sermon, 3,000 who had rejected Christ two months earlier now repented, receiving Him as Savior and Lord. This catch far exceeded the number of fish caught when Peter's nets were miraculously full at the order of Jesus to launch out or let down. Someone commented, "It took one sermon to win 3,000. Today it takes 3,000 sermons to win one soul." Jesus had promised that His disciples would do greater miracles than He.

Since God's program moves ahead according to schedule, just as Jesus was born in the fullness of time, so the Spirit came when the day of Pentecost was fully come (Acts 2:1). Pentecost, meaning *fifty,* stands for the 50th day after Passover when the first fruits of harvest were offered in gratitude to God's goodness.

Suddenly the explosive sound of a mighty rushing wind filled the house where the 120 were sitting, causing crowds to rush together. A ball of fire, separating into individual tongues, hovered over each of the 120. Filled with the Spirit, each disciple began to speak in a dialect which he normally did not talk. People heard in their own vernacular of the wonderful works of God, including the redemptive death and resurrection of Christ. Perhaps a disciple would confront a stranger, speaking in that foreigner's mother tongue, whether Egyptian, Arabian, or whatever of the sixteen different countries specifically mentioned (Acts 2:8–11).

Some think this was a miracle of hearing, not of speaking. But in that case would not the fiery symbol have been ears instead of tongues, and would not then have rested on the hearers instead of on the speakers.

The normal population of Jerusalem swelled considerably at this most popular of all feasts. Through this divine strategy the seed of the Gospel was carried back and planted in many quarters of the Roman Empire.

Some accused the disciples of intoxication. At this pivotal point Peter used the miracle as a spring-board for a sermon. Denying that the disciples were drunk, for it was too early in the day for that, he affirmed the miracle was a fulfillment of an Old Testament prophecy spoken by Joel (2:16–21).

Referring back to Jesus of Nazareth and his many miracles, Peter boldly charged his hearers with His crucifixion. Not to lessen their guilt, but to help explain how the Messiah could die so shamefully, Peter placed the cross in the sovereign plan of God. By the determinate counsel of God, their wicked hands had crucified Him (2:22,23).

But, continued Peter, God raised up Jesus from the dead. His resurrection was predicted by David (Psalms 16:8–11). Furthermore, Jesus has ascended into heaven and been exalted at the right hand of God. This too was prophesied by David (Psalms 110:1).

Peter then explained the miracle of the tongues. The risen, exalted Jesus "hath shed forth this, which ye now see and hear" (Acts 2:33).

Stricken in conscience, his audience saw that their sentence against Jesus had been reversed by a higher court. They had condemned Him. But God had made Him both Lord and Christ (2:36). The One they crucified was now alive and the Lord of glory. All they had to do to silence this bold Peter was to produce the body of Jesus. But hundreds of them had doubtless visited the empty tomb and were convinced of the truth spoken by Peter.

Under deep conviction, they asked Peter and the rest of the apostles, "Men and brethren, what shall we do?" (2:37). Peter told them to repent, which meant a change of mind. They had to reverse their view of Jesus, acknowledging Him as their Messiah. When Rembrandt painted the crucifixion, he put himself in the crowd. To be saved, we must confess that our sins helped nail Him to the cross, then acknowledge Him as our risen Savior and Lord.

As an outward sign of their inward commitment, Peter told them to be baptized in the name of Jesus Christ. Such confession of the name they had so recently and shamefully mistreated would require great courage. Baptism is an open declaration of our inward identification with the death and resurrection of Christ. But it's that inward faith (as evidenced in the outer symbol of baptism) that brings remission of sins and the gift of the Holy Spirit (2:37,38).

Peter's bold preaching netted 3,000 baptized believers. From this beginning of new life in Christ, they continued steadfast in the apostles' teaching, in fellowship, in breaking of bread, in prayers, in sharing, and in praising God. The result of their perseverance, devotion, love, and liberality was daily addition of new souls to the church.

The Peter of Pentecost was radically different from the Simon of the high priest's courtyard. What changed him from a denier to a declarer?

THE MOTIVATED APOSTLE

Men have been known to grow twenty years in one short hour. Though Peter grew steadily and slowly during the three-year earthly ministry of Christ, he took tremendous strides forward in the fifty-day period from the resurrection to Pentecost. What were the factors that caused this major advance of character in less than two months?

The Hope of the Resurrection

Peter had seen Jesus hanging on the cross and knew He had been buried in Joseph of Arimithea's tomb. Had that been the end, the followers of Jesus would have been of all men most miserable.

But Christ rose victoriously from the grave. Peter had seen the risen Christ, not once, but repeatedly. He knew that because Christ lived, he too would live. Come what may—whatever the Sanhedrin or persecuting countrymen might do to him, even if it meant crucifixion some day like his Master—Peter knew that he would return from the grave and live eternally. Death held no fear for Peter.

The thrill of seeing His Lord back from the dead propelled Peter to bold witness. Peter couldn't keep the good news of Christ's rising to himself. The truth burned like fire in his heart. He had to shout it out. To thousands at Pentecost he proclaimed, "This Jesus hath God raised up, whereof we are all witnesses" (Acts 2:32). Then to the crowd on Solomon's porch after the healing of the lame man, to the Sanhedrin, to the household of Cornelius, he pealed forth the same exciting evangel, "Christ rose from the dead."

The miracle of the empty tomb was a major factor in the dramatic behavior change in all the apostles. So strongly did they believe this that nothing short of death could stop their witness. To silence his preaching, Luke, according to tradition, was hanged on an olive tree. James, brother of Jesus, who once ridiculed Jesus, was beaten, stoned, and had his brains dashed out by a club. Mark was dragged to pieces by an angry mob. *Martyr* means witness.

A skilled doctor died of a heart attack. His widow, deeply in love with him, bore up well during the funeral. People thought she would break down when reaction set in. But to everyone's amazement her spirits continued buoyant. One day, when some friends asked her secret, she led them down the hall to the doctor's reception room. Snapping on the light she pointed to a sign hanging on a doorknob of his office. Then they understood. The widow explained, "The maid forgot to remove the sign. She put all the rest of the rooms in order, but perhaps the Lord let her leave it here. Right after his death I spotted the hand-lettered sign, hanging a little unevenly, just as he had left it. That message gave me the courage to go on." The sign read, "Gone for a little while. Will be with you soon."

Peter later wrote, "Blessed be the God and Father of our Lord Jesus Christ, which according to his abundant mercy hath begotten us again unto a lively hope by the resurrection of Jesus Christ from the dead" (I Peter 1:3). Several versions translate it "a living hope."

Because He lives, like Peter we can face tomorrow.

The Enlightenment of Scripture

Another key factor in Peter's new behavior was a proper understanding of the Scriptures. A year before, when Jesus had foretold His coming sufferings and death in Jerusalem, Peter had rebuked Jesus for talking so. In turn, Jesus had called Peter's reaction offensive.

But now Peter had come into a new comprehension of the Word. Not only had he heard Moses and Elijah, representatives of the Old Testament Law and Prophets discussing the death of Jesus, but after the resurrection he had had the personal instruction of Jesus Christ. In the upper room on the first Easter night, the Master had explained how the law of Moses, the Prophets, and the Psalms all predicted His sufferings and resurrection. The necessity of both cross and crown in God's plan of redemption illuminated their minds.

During that forty-day post-resurrection span Jesus had not only appeared to His disciples but had also elaborated on Old Testament prophecies. No wonder the apostles could so often write that certain events happened that "it might be fulfilled that which was spoken by the prophet saying . . ." Peter had been a pupil in the greatest course ever offered in Old Testament interpretation.

Significantly, at least half of Peter's recorded Pentecostal sermon is comprised of quotations from the Old Testament: Joel 2:28–32; Psalms 16:8–11; and Psalms 110:1. In all of his recorded sermons Peter makes references to the Old Testament, for example, Acts 3:18, 21–26; 4:11,12; 10:43. A greater grasp of scriptural truth emboldened Peter.

The Power of the Spirit

Undoubtedly, the major element in making a new Peter was the coming of the Holy Spirit at Pentecost. If Christ needed to begin His ministry in the power of the Spirit after His baptism and temptation, how much more did Peter need the Spirit's anointing (Luke 4:14).

The Lord promised the apostles the Holy Spirit to "teach you all things, and bring all things to your remembrance, whatsoever I have said unto you" (John 14:26). When Peter was on trial before the Sanhedrin, it was the power of the Spirit that told him what to say in his defense.

It was also the Holy Spirit Who gave Peter boldness to speak. It is with good reason that wine and the Holy Spirit often found in the same biblical context. For example, John the Baptist was not to drink strong drink or wine, but would be filled with the Spirit from birth. Also, on Pentecost, the followers of Christ were thought to be under the influence of wine when in reality they were under the power of the Holy Ghost. A familiar text reads, "Be not drunk with wine, but be filled with the Spirit" (Ephesians 5:18). Just as the wrong kind of spirits often makes timid

people courageous, and quiet folks talkative, so the Holy
Spirit made Peter, who formerly cowed before one maid,
now speak openly before thousands of people, proclaiming
the person and work of Christ.

How fearlessly Peter defended himself against the rulers. Though forbidden to teach in the name of Jesus, he
continued to do so. The assembled church, praying over
this matter, "were all filled with the Holy Ghost, and they
spake the word of God with boldness" (Acts 4:31).

Only the power of the Spirit could account for the fantastic results at Jerusalem. Was anything more absurd than
for a lowly band of people, like those assembled in the upper
room, to think their efforts could make any impression on
the unreceptive pagan world? Their leader had been crucified
and His grave had been sealed with an official Roman seal.

But then God shook the city. Before long the disciples
numbered 5,000 plus. The energy of the Spirit had worked
through Peter and the others.

To be new men and women we need to same Holy-
Ghost unction.

The Grace of Forgiveness

The final motivating factor in Peter's new life was
Christ's forgiveness toward him. As explained in the previous chapter, poor Peter had thought all was finished after
the crowing of the cock and the lamentable look the Master
gave him as He was led away. Could he ever be forgiven
for denying he ever knew Jesus, and for such strong, repeated, blasphemous denials? But after three nights of almost
unbearable remorse, the Master met him privately, forgave
him, then restored him in the presence of other disciples.
Gratitude for Christ's abundant grace motivated him to bold
witness.

An elder in a Canadian church, slipping back for the first time in ten years to his pre-conversion, besetting sin of intoxication, made a fool of himself on a crowded city streetcar. Ashamed of his drunken behavior, and aware that he had been recognized by many Christians and non-Christians, he stopped attending church, despite attempts to restore him. He was removed from the elder board. However, the Lord dealt with him, so that before long he came to the midweek meeting and openly confessed his sin. He was soon voted back onto the elder board. Remarkably, the board voted to purge from its minutes every mention of the incident, so that today no record of the matter exists anywhere on the church books. That restored elder, like Peter motivated by the grace of forgiveness, resumed his Christian service as though he were a new man.

11

Bulwark to the Brethren

The *Peter Principle,* a theory popular in business management a few years ago, contends that people rise to the level of their incompetency. According to this thesis, any person, repeatedly promoted, is bound to reach a level of responsibility beyond his ability.

In the case of the Apostle Peter, the Lord prayed that despite his denial he would reach the place, after his restoration, where he would strengthen his brethren (Luke 22:32). In those stirring opening chapters of Acts, Peter, a renewed man, rose to the level of divinely empowered competency to fulfill the destiny for which the Master had called him. As a miracle-worker, a disciplinarian, and an evangelist, he proved himself a bulwark to his fellow-believers.

MIRACLE-WORKER

Of all apostolic characters in the first dozen chapters of Acts only the name of Peter is connected with specific miracles. Though wonders were performed by the other apostles and by deacons elected to help the apostolic band, no particular miracle is recounted of any of these, except for Ananias in the healing of Paul's blindness (Acts 2:43; 5:12–16; 6:8; 8:6,13). The few particular miracles in which people are named are linked to Peter.

Lame Man in Jerusalem (Acts 3)

Peter was involved in the first recorded, specific miracle of the early church, probably selected because it led to a collision with the authorities and Peter's first imprisonment.

A man crippled from birth was begging at his usual spot in front of the temple gate called Beautiful. The crowd was starting to come for the 3:00 p.m. prayer time, among them, Peter and John.

A close friendship existed between these two disciples. Peter and John were partners in a fishing business (Luke 5:10). They had been converted around the same time, called by Christ at the same time, with James had been together as members of the inner three, were probably partners when sent out two-by-two, had prepared the Passover together in the upper room (Luke 22:8), had been together in the high priest's courtyard, and would be in jail together. In this friendship John's pensiveness and Peter's activism provided a healthy balance.

Seeing these two, the cripple asked for alms. Peter said to the beggar, "Look on us." The beggar looked, expecting some gift. Imagine his disappointment when he heard Peter say, "Silver and gold have I none." What a poor joke, thought the lame man. Then he heard Peter say, "In the name of Jesus Christ of Nazareth rise up and walk."

Poverty need not keep us from doing good. People may be helped by ways other than money. A little girl whose mother had just died was given a ten-dollar bill by a well-meaning neighbor. After the neighbor left, the girl threw the bill on the floor in frustration. Another neighbor, coming in moments later, cradled the girl in her arms till she fell asleep in a much needed rest.

The cripple discovered that some things are better than money. He who had to be carried from place to place now received strength in his feet and ankle bones (words used only by Luke in the New Testament). He stood, walked, then leaped and shouted praises to God.

As his praises rang through the temple area, people gathered round, amazed at this genuine, powerful miracle. The man, over 40, had been seen there for years. The disease was from birth. The cure was not performed in secret, but before a daytime crowd. Unfriendly authorities later admitted the case genuine (Acts 4:14–16).

Peter the opportunist used the miracle as a springboard for a witness. He disclaimed all credit for the miracle and turned their attention to Jesus whom they delivered up to death, but whom God honored by raising from the dead. It was faith in Christ that has given soundness to this lame man, Peter said. Incidentally, this miracle should have made the populace think of Jesus, for He had healed both lame and blind in this very same temple area just a few weeks before during "holy week" (Matthew 21:14).

Peter softened up the charge of crucifixion against them by stating they did it out of ignorance, that it was in the predicted plan of God. But they needed to repent in order to have their sins blotted out. As in all his sermons Peter quoted several Old Testament verses. As a result, Peter and John were imprisoned.

The Shadow of Peter (Acts 5:12–16)

In its early days, before its ordeal of persecution, the church was given much public favor, largely because of the miraculous works of healing. The authority of the apostles was greatly strengthened by these wonders, most of which were wrought by their hands (Acts 5:12; 2 Corinthians 12:12).

Multitudes, attracted from the neighboring countryside, brought their ill to be healed. Just as people had sought to touch the hem of Christ's garment for healing, so now

folks placed their sick on the narrow streets of Jerusalem
so that the shadow of Peter passing by might be cast on
their bed-mats (Matthew 14:35,36).

Did Peter's shadow actually heal? G. Campbell Morgan
comments, "First of all notice that the paragraph does not
say that the shadow of Peter healed any one of them, or
that it did not. . . . The phrase 'the shadow of Peter' is a
purely Eastern phrase; and in the Eastern lands today people
will try to escape from the shadow of one man because
there is an evil influence supposed to be in it; and they
will try to come into the shadow of another in which there
is supposed to be an influence for good. This is purely an
Eastern picture, but see what it reveals; and see what these
men thought of Peter. Sick people felt they would be healed
if put in his shadow. It is a revelation of these people's
conception of the power of the Christian Church" (*Acts of
the Apostles,* Revell, 1924, p. 155).

Perhaps the shadow didn't heal, but instead helped people have faith for healing. On the other hand, Christ could
have healed as easily by a shadow as by a word or touch.

Miracles in Judea

When persecution hit the church at Jerusalem, scat-
tering believers throughout all regions of Judea and Samaria,
Peter and the apostles stuck out the tough going at Jerusalem. Later Peter made trips to brethren in nearby regions.
On one of these tours Peter performed two miracles.

One he did while ministering to the saints at Lydda,
called Lud today, located two-thirds of the way between
Jerusalem and the seaport Joppa. There Peter came across
a sick believer, Aeneas, same name as the hero of Virgil's
Aeneid which means *praise.* Luke noted he had been par-
alyzed and bedridden for eight years (Acts 9:33).

Peter said to Aeneas, "Jesus Christ maketh thee whole: arise, and make thy bed" (vs. 34). Immediately he arose, and rolled up the bed-mat on which he had been carried those many years. When news of this cure spread through the city and to the neighboring coastal area, many turned from their old, sinful ways to the new ways of the Lord.

Nine miles west of Lydda in Joppa, known also as Jaffa, and existing today next to the modern seaport of Tel-Aviv, lived a believer named Dorcas. Deeply loved, she was "full of good works and almsdeeds," but that God would be glorified she became sick and died. Hearing Peter was at Lydda, the believers in Joppa sent two men asking him to hurry back with them. Arriving, he was ushered into the upper chamber where "all the widows stood by him weeping, and shewing the coats and garments which Dorcas made" (vs. 39). Her dedicated needle has inspired countless Dorcas sewing societies in churches down through the centuries.

Like his Master in healing Jairus, Peter performed the miracle in privacy, putting all the people out. Kneeling and praying, he turned toward the corpse, "Tabitha (Aramaic for *Dorcas*), arise." Dorcas opened her eyes and sat up. Peter reached out his hand, lifted her up, and presented her alive to the saints.

Sign gifts seem to have been given for those difficult, early days of the infant church. Who would believe the word of these ignorant and unlearned men with their fantastic story of one who rose from the dead? The apostles were not left discredited. Their miracles authenticated them. With the completion of the New Testament need for such credentials diminished. Should the gift of miracles be assigned by the Spirit today, several writers suggest it would likely occur on mission fields where the situation approximates that of the early church. Missionaries sometimes report such instances, reminiscent of apostolic history.

DISCIPLINARIAN

Because of these miracles done through the power of Christ, Peter was indeed a bulwark to the brethren. But he also was a tower of strength through his discipline of hypocritical believers.

Ananias and Sapphira (Acts 5:1–11)

So strongly were the early saints motivated by love for their brethren that they willingly shared their assets, some even selling property and possessions to help those in need. This practice was voluntary, operating on the Christian principle, "What is mine is thine," but could it happen again today if the need arose? Though the rich felt their things should be shared with the poor, nothing is said about the poor thinking that what belonged to their rich brethren was theirs.

The rich were free to retain their property, like Barnabas' sister, Mary, in whose home the church met (Acts 12:12). Or they could sell it and give the proceeds to the church, like Barnabas, who sold his land on Cyprus and laid the money at the apostles' feet (4:36,37).

Inspired by Barnabas' magnaminity, a husband and wife, Ananias and Sapphira, talked over selling some property. Only outwardly did their deed seem the same as Barnabas's. After selling the property, the couple kept back part of the sale price, gave the rest, but told Peter they had given all. They wanted a reputation for generosity greater than what was due them. Envious of Barnabas, they wanted their names on the church-giving honor roll. Do we generate more credit for our spirituality, prayerfulness, or generosity than we actually practice?

Though others may have been saying, "Isn't that so nice of brother Ananias? Isn't he generous?" Peter didn't approve, but with the gift of discernment rebuked him strongly. "Why hath Satan filled thine heart to lie to the Holy Ghost, and to keep back part of the price of the land?" Ananias' act was a deliberate, defiant lie. He didn't have to sell the property. He willfully thought this plan up. He could have kept part of the sale price, as he did. But to keep it, while all the time pretending he gave all, was a lie. The couple tried to serve two masters, pride and money.

Hearing these words, Ananias fell down and died, judgment falling not on a murderer or adulterer, but on a respectable man who falsified a church donation.

Burial was immediate in that culture. Three hours later Sapphira came looking for her husband. Arriving, she expected to hear, "Sister, what a wonderful gift you and your husband gave. You certainly are doing a lot for the Lord. You'll be greatly rewarded at the judgment seat of Christ."

But instead Peter asked her the amount of the sale price of the land. The money Ananias brought may have still been at Peter's feet. He probed her conscience to give her a chance to repent. But she brazenly repeated the same lie as her husband and suffered the same doom. What marriage unity! The couple was one in hypocrisy, one in death, and one in the grave, and one in the record of the Bible which has been read by millions.

Great fear came on all. If God were to strike down every saint who acted hypocritically, churches would be empty. The Lord did this unique thing to emphasize the seriousness of sin and the need for holiness before Him.

Sin in the thought life soon makes itself known in the outer world. The story is told of a king who used to make all the kings he conquered bow to him in a public ceremony. One conquered king, who didn't want his subservience a matter of public viewing, asked for the bowing ceremony to be done privately inside the king's tent. At the height of the private ceremony the reigning king, through the pulling of tent ropes at a prearranged signal, stripped his tent of all covering to reveal the conquered king on his knees before his conqueror. Bowing to some vice privately will soon be found out, as Ananias and Sapphira discovered.

Simon the Sorcerer (Acts 8:9–24)

If people today succumb to fortune-tellers and occultists, think how susceptible first-century Christians were to superstition. In Samaria, a magician by the name of Simon, a clever, unscrupulous charlatan, had long bewitched the people from the least to the greatest, calling himself the great power of God. When Philip the evangelist conducted a crusade in Samaria, people responded to the Gospel, much impressed by the evangelist's miracles. Simon the sorcerer also believed and submitted to baptism.

Since up to now only Jews had become believers, such a divergence as baptizing despised Samaritans needed apostolic approval. On arrival, Peter and John prayed that the Samaritans might receive the Holy Spirit. When sorcerer Simon saw the manifestation of the Holy Spirit as a result of the laying on of hands by Peter and John, he offered the apostles money, saying "Give me also this power, that on whomsoever I lay hands, he may receive the Holy Ghost." What prestige and wealth would be his if he could reproduce this trick. He put the operation of the Holy Spirit on a level with pulling a rabbit out of a hat. His name has given rise to a word that describes the buying or selling of ecclesiastical preferment—simony.

Again exercising his gift of discernment, Peter rebuked him, "Thy money perish with thee, because thou hast thought that the gift of God may be purchased with money." Peter continued, "Thou hast neither part nor lot in this matter: for thy heart is not right in the sight of God. Repent therefore of this thy wickedness, and pray God, if perhaps the thought of thine heart may be forgiven thee. For I perceive that thou art in the gall of bitterness, and in the bond of iniquity."

To this appeal to restoration Simon, terror-stricken at incurring divine displeasure, asked prayer on his behalf so that none of these things would come upon him.

Though some think Simon was never regenerated, some evidence does exist to indicate he was a converted man who backslid. Luke, who penned this story some years after it happened, says Simon believed and was baptized. Peter's counsel to repent and pray was not advice normally given a non-Christian but was suitable for a backslider. If Simon asked Peter to pray for him, it was likely Simon would also pray himself. One version (Codex Bezae) adds that the sorcerer, "Who weeping much, did not cease." If Simon did repent, he had the edifying teaching of Peter and John "who testified and preached the word of the Lord before returning to Jerusalem."

Again it was Peter who strengthened the brethren as a disciplinarian by protecting the person and work of the Holy Spirit.

EVANGELIST (Acts 10)

Jesus had commanded the disciples to be witnesses not only in Jerusalem, Judea and Samaria, but to the ends of the earth. Peter was instrumental in bringing the Gospel to the Jews in Jerusalem, then to the Samaritans, and then to the Gentiles in the household of Cornelius. Peter was involved in each major step of evangelism.

The admittance of Gentiles into the church as part of God's plan was well known. "God so loved the world" would certainly include them. The Great Commission ordered preaching to all nations. But how Gentiles were to be admitted was the problem—through Judaism or apart from

Judaism? Cornelius would become the first Gentile convert admitted without submitting to Jewish rites. This episode would rock the church to its very foundation, initiating a controversy which would necessitate the first church council, and which would involve much of Paul's time and energy for years to come.

Cornelius was a devout centurion stationed in Caesarea, thirty miles north of Joppa. He feared God, gave much alms to the people, fasted often, and prayed to God regularly. But still he needed the Gospel.

Peter—Human Instrument

Cornelius saw in a vision an angel who told him that his prayers and alms had come for a memorial before God, and that he should send men to Joppa to call for one Simon, whose surname was Peter, who was lodging with another Simon, a tanner. This Simon Peter would have a message for Cornelius. When the angel departed, Cornelius appointed two of his household servants and a devout soldier to hunt Peter up in Joppa.

Why didn't the angel preach the Gospel to Cornelius instead of having him send for Peter to come and preach the Gospel? How less complicated if, instead of sending three men on this 30-mile trip each way to secure Peter, the angel could have gathered Cornelius' household together right there and then, and given the same message Peter would give.

The answer is simple. Angels cannot preach the Gospel, though they would delight to do so. They know full well of the sinfulness of mankind, of the incarnation and death of Christ as the price for redemption, of the need to carry this good news to the ends of the earth. But they are denied this privilege. Though the word "evangelize" means to announce good news, the assignment of announcing good news has been restricted to redeemed people. Believers are the ones who must "ev-*angel*ize." So, the angel had Cornelius send for Peter.

Peter Prepared

Next day at noon, as the three servants were on their way toward him, Peter was praying on the flat housetop of the tanner's home, the quietest spot in an eastern domicile. To prepare Peter for the preaching mission in Cornelius' home, the Lord gave him a vision of a giant sheet descending from heaven, containing both clean and unclean animals. A voice told Peter to rise and eat, to which he responded, "Not so, Lord; for I have never eaten anything that is common or unclean." The voice replied, "What God hath cleansed, that call not thou common." The command was repeated three times before the sheet was lifted back to heaven. A little bit of the old Peter seemed to creep in at this point in his slowness to grasp a divine lesson.

Wondering what it all meant, Peter was told by the Spirit that three men were at the door, seeking him. He was to go with them, not doubting, for they were sent by God. When Peter answered the door and learned their mission, he began to understand the meaning of the vision. He lodged them overnight, then went with them to Caesarea, taking six believers with him (Acts 11:12).

Cornelius welcomed and worshiped Peter, who objected to his worship, saying, "Stand up; I myself am a man." Finding many assembled in the house, Peter said, "Ye know how that it is an unlawful thing for a man that is a Jew to keep company, or come unto one of another nation; but God hath shewed me that I should not call any man common or unclean. Therefore came I unto you without gainsaying,

as soon as I was sent for: I ask therefore for what intent
ye have sent for me?" The recent vision had solved in Peter's
mind the admissibility of Gentiles into the church.

Then Cornelius related his story, concluding, "Now
therefore are we all here present before God, to hear all
things that are commanded thee of God."

Peter Preaching

Peter began with the recognition that God is no re-
specter of persons but will receive people of every nation.
Racial difference is no barrier to soul-winning. All men are
acceptable candidates for salvation. Peter spoke of Jesus of
Nazareth who went about doing good, then of His death
and resurrection of which Peter was a witness. Then Peter
reached the climax, "whosoever believeth in him shall receive remission of sins."

At that point, while Peter was still preaching, the Holy
Spirit fell on all of them. The six Jewish brethren who had
come with Paul were astonished because that on the Gentiles
was poured out the gift of the Holy Spirit, enabling the
new believers to speak with tongues and magnify God.

Peter's action caused some scandal back in Jerusalem.
Had Peter been absolute leader of the church, he would
never have allowed his brethren to call him to account, nor
would he have had to plead his case at their bar. How wise
he had been to take along those six Jewish brethren who
now backed up his every word (Acts 11:12). When the Jerusalem leaders heard his account, "they held their peace,
and glorified God, saying, Then hath God also to the Gentiles granted repentance unto life" (vs. 18). It was Peter
who first brought the Gospel to the Jews, Samaritans, and
Gentiles.

The Lord still uses human instruments to proclaim the
Gospel to both Jew and Gentile. In an imaginary scene in

heaven right after the Ascension, the angel Gabriel is chatting with the ascended Lord, "Master, you died for all peoples of the world, did you not?"

"Yes, I did."

"You must have suffered very much."

"Yes, Gabriel."

"And do they all know about it down there?"

"Oh, no. Just a little handful in Galilee and Jerusalem know about it thus far."

"Well, Master, what plan have you made so all the world will hear?"

The Master answered, "Well, I asked Peter and James and John and some more down there to make it the business of their lives to tell others. And the others to tell others, till the last man in the farthest part has heard the story, all the way from Jerusalem, Judea, and Samaria, to the ends of the earth."

Gabriel's brow knits, for he thinks he spots a flaw in the Master's plan. "Yes, Master, but suppose, after a while Peter forgets and goes back to his fishing. Suppose John, after a bit, loses his enthusiasm, and just doesn't tell others. Suppose their successors down in the twentieth century get so busy with things, even good things like church matters, that they do not tell the others, what then?"

Back comes the quiet voice of the Lord Jesus, "Gabriel, I haven't made any other plans."

12

Under Fire

John Bunyan spent 13 years in jail for the crime of preaching the Gospel outside the established church of England. But according to one historian, he was granted a fair amount of liberty by his jailers. Often allowed out of prison overnight, he preached in the village or woods, even visiting friends in London on one occasion. When the magistrate heard this, Bunyan was not permitted to look out the door of the jail. When this ruling wore off, he again had the opportunity of visiting groups to preach by stealth. Reportedly, many of the Baptist congregations in Bedforshire owe their origin to his midnight preaching.

On one such occasion when his jailer had granted permission for an all-night visit, Bunyan began to feel uneasy late in the evening, so returned to prison before midnight. A nearby magistrate, informed that Bunyan had broken out of prison, sent a messenger to be a witness against the merciful jailer. On arrival he demanded, "Let me see John Bunyan." Bunyan was called up to confront the astonished messenger. Later his kind jailer said to Bunyan, "You may leave whenever you want, for you seem to know much better when to return than I can tell you."

Like Bunyan, Peter was unjustly imprisoned for preaching the Gospel. And like Bunyan, Peter was released from jail, on two occasions at least. Peter's releases, however, were due directly to angelic intervention.

PETER'S FIRST IMPRISONMENT
(Acts 4:1–31)

Up to now in *Acts* we've had the first sermon, the first New Testament church, the first miracle, and now we have the first persecution. The Master had told His disciples, "The servant is not greater than his lord. If they have persecuted me, they will also persecute you" (John 15:20). Jesus certainly suffered persecution. Now we have the beginning of oppression for the apostles.

God prepared His servants for suffering by degrees. This first persecution was just imprisonment overnight. The second one involved overnight jailing plus a beating. Then martyrdom came for Stephen and James. Though Peter was again imprisoned, a miraculous escape enabled him to proclaim the Gospel and strengthen the brethren for a couple more decades. However, he also became a martyr for his faith. At first Peter resisted to bonds, then later to a beating, then finally to blood. Lesser trials prepared him for greater ones.

Arrest

Such a crowd gathered at the miracle of the lame man to hear the preaching of Peter that the temple authorities intervened, spurred on mostly by the Sadducees, the most powerful but least orthodox party. The Sadduccees were grieved on two counts. First, that the apostles taught the people, a privilege the Sadduccees wanted only for themselves. Second, that the apostles taught the resurrection of Jesus from the dead, which ran counter to the anti-supernaturalism of the Sadducees who rejected miracles, angels, and the resurrection. So they arrested Peter and John and put them in jail. Peter had boasted he would follow Jesus to prison. Now this became a reality.

Every saint will encounter opposition, animosity, or tribulation at some time or other because of his witness. But through trials the work of God can march triumphantly forward. Though the apostles were confined, the word of God was not. Apparently, hundreds more believed, bringing the total up to 5,000 (Acts 4:4). These new believers embraced the faith with eyes open to the danger of persecution.

Arraignment

Next morning the leaders convened. A few weeks earlier these same members of the Sanhedrin had met to discuss the fate of Jesus. Though they thought they had gotten rid of Him, He now came back to haunt them in the message of Peter. The risen Christ was still working through His apostles.

When the Sanhedrin filed into their seats, Peter and John, led in from their cell, were placed in the center of a semicircle, facing the presiding officer who asked them, "By what power have ye done this?" The emphatic word is *ye*. "How could unlearned, contemptible men like you do this?"

Answer

Peter had no prepared defense. He experienced the fulfillment of Jesus' command not to prepare an answer in advance for the Holy Spirit would tell them in that hour what to say (Luke 12:11,12). (This promise is not for Sunday school teachers or preachers but for those hailed before courts for the Gospel's sake.)

Peter began his defense with a little humor, saying in effect, "If we are being examined regarding the healing of this lame man, it's a little absurd to try us as criminals when all we have done is a good deed."

Though on the defense, Peter went to the attack. He declared that the lame man, standing there as exhibit A, was healed by Jesus of Nazareth, Whom, he charged, they crucified, but Whom God raised from the dead. Peter then likened Christ to the "stone which the builders refused is become the headstone of the corner" (Psalm 118:22).

A few weeks earlier Peter had been afraid of one female servant of these high priests. Now he spoke with Holy Ghost boldness to the entire Sanhedrin, the same men who had so recently condemned Jesus and who could easily do the same to him.

But Peter wasn't through. Not only did he tell the Sanhedrin that this man's healing came through Jesus, but also that from Jesus alone comes salvation. "Neither is there salvation in any other: for there is none other name under heaven given among men, whereby we must be saved" (Acts 4:12). Though today many claim that there are numerous paths to God, that youthful generation of believers who pointed a lone finger upward as a symbol of salvation were right—there's only one way. Peter emphasized Christianity's exclusivism.

Admonition

The boldness, plus the competency in the Old Testament, of these unschooled men amazed the authorities. They recognized that they had been with Jesus. To prepare for his role as Albert Einstein, an actor went to great lengths to represent the great scientist adequately. He secured a tape of Einstein's acceptance speech when awarded the Nobel Prize in 1942, and a tape of an interview made in his home in Princeton. He listened to the tapes hundreds of times to pick up the tones, accents, nuances, and little hesitations. He would listen to the tapes before going to bed, and in the morning felt he was getting up with Albert Einstein. How wonderful if people could tell from our speech and behavior that we had been with Jesus. We need to take the time to meditate in the word and pray. The hymnwriter says,

> *"Take time to be holy, the world rushes on;*
> *Much time spend in secret with Jesus alone;*
> *By looking to Jesus, like Him thou shalt be;*
> *Thy friends in thy conduct His likeness shall*
>   *see."*

Sending the apostles aside, the Sanhedrin conferred among themselves. No law had been broken. Rather, a notable miracle had been performed, making the defendants heroes. To punish them would be poor politics, but to let them go on spreading the name of Jesus would be unwise. So, recalling Peter and John, they dismissed them with the order not to speak nor teach in His name.

The apostles declared their intent to defy the ban, and to continue speaking the things they had seen and heard. Peter taught in his epistle that Christians are to normally obey government. However, when obedience to government means disobedience to God, God is to be obeyed.

Despite the apostolic defiance, the Sanhedrin did nothing but repeat their threat. Popular enthusiasm may have deterred them from doing more. Peter and John returned to their own group, reported their experience, and went to prayer. The place was shaken. Filled with the Holy Spirit, they continued to speak the word of God with boldness.

Aftermath

In a Virginia suburb, a little mission church was established in a growing fashionable neighborhood. As costly residences were erected near the church, some owners became disturbed by the enthusiastic singing. Getting up a petition of neighbors for a zoning ordinance to get rid of the church, they went to a Jew for his signature. To their surprise he pushed the petition away, saying, "Gentlemen, I cannot sign it. If I believed as these Christians that my Messiah had come, I would shout it from every housetop in this suburb, and no one could stop me."

PETER'S SECOND IMPRISONMENT (Acts 5:17–42)

Like the earlier jailing, an arrest late in the day is followed by a night in prison, arraignment before the Council, a sermon by Peter, a warning, a refusal to obey, and renewed enthusiasm. Only this time two elements are added: first, temporary angelic release from prison, and second, a beating. The persecution increased in intensity. This episode could be captioned, "Beaten, but unbowed."

Reason for Jailing

What led to the arrest was the increasing tempo of the witness to Jesus Christ. The Sadducees had ordered a ban on speaking in His name, but now that name was filling all Jerusalem, so that believers were added, multitudes both of men and women. So, the Sanhedrin, filled with envy and indignation, swooped down on the apostles and put them in the common prison.

Release

Before dawn an angel opened the prison doors, led the apostles out, and commanded them to go stand in the temple and speak all the words of life. The following scene had its humor. The Sanhedrin convened and sent for the prisoners. But though the prison doors were shut and the guards in place, upon opening up the doors the officers found no one inside. So while the Sanhedrin sat ready in all its splendor and dignity with no prisoner to question, word reached them the apostles were nearby, standing in the temple and teaching the people that name which the Sanhedrin had forbidden them to mention.

The temple officers persuaded the apostles to come voluntarily. Otherwise a nasty scene could have erupted.

Defense

The high priest reminded the apostles of their previous command, expostulating about their violation, thus filling Jerusalem with apostolic doctrine and making the Sanhedrin responsible for Jesus' death.

Filled with the Spirit, spokesman Peter charged them (the leaders, not the Jews in general) with Jesus' death. He contrasted God's treatment of Christ with the Sanhedrin's. They hanged Christ on a tree; God exalted Him to His right hand to be a Prince and a Savior. He ended by claiming the apostles were witnesses of Christ's death and resurrection.

Verdict

Peter's defense was not designed to win friends and influence people. So enraged was the Sanhedrin that they considered a death sentence. But an eminent teacher, Gamaliel, cautioned against rash action. Citing recent insurrections which soon perished, he advised no action, for time would tell. If of men, the apostolic movement would come to an end. But if of God, they could not possibly overthrow it. Why didn't Gamaliel ask for an investigation of Peter's claims?

The respected doctor's advice prevailed. But too angry

to let the apostles go without punishment, the Council had them flogged, presumably the 40 stripes minus one. Then they repeated their earlier order—do not speak in the name of Jesus.

Reaction

If many modern believers were so treated, they would have reacted, "Is this our reward for faithfully preaching Christ? We quit!" Or they might have reasoned, "God isn't with us anymore. Last night He released us from prison, but today He has forsaken us, for He let us be beaten!"

But note the reaction of the apostles, "And they departed from the presence of the council, rejoicing that they were counted worthy to suffer shame for his name." The beating prepared them for future persecution, teaching that God does not always rescue His own from every trial, but will always give grace sufficient to endure.

Did they stop mentioning the name of Jesus? "And daily in the temple, and in every house, they ceased not to teach and preach Jesus Christ."

When Bunyan was once sentenced to three months for preaching the Gospel outside the established Church of England, and threatened with banishment if he did not promise to abstain from such preaching, he replied, "If I were out of prison today, I would preach the Gospel again tomorrow, by the help of God."

A Navy officer, mistakenly arrested with a group of Communists demonstrating against NATO during Eisenhower's visit to Paris in the '40s, spent three hours in jail before he convinced authorities he was not a communist. He was amazed at the way the Communists behaved. In jail they began to sing and shout because they were so thrilled with the privilege of suffering for Communism. Said the officer, "We who are Christians need to have the same devotion to Jesus Christ. Are we willing to sacrifice ease, comfort, and luxury to stand up for the name of Christ?"

PETER'S THIRD IMPRISONMENT
(Acts 12:1–19)

Herod Agrippa I, grandson of Herod the Great, infamous for his massacre of the infants at Jesus' birth, and only here mentioned in the New Testament, was cruel, bloodthirsty, and fond of public display. In his eagerness to ingratiate himself to the Jews, he beheaded James, brother of John.

Arrest

Seeing that the death of James pleased the Jews, Herod proceeded to arrest Peter also, their evident leader and top prize. Since it was Passover, great numbers of Jews would have come to Jerusalem, thus adding to Herod's popularity.

Peter was kept in jail with the intent of public trial immediately after the holiday. The people were anticipating a great spectacle. Everyone had heard of Peter. First he would be sentenced, then killed.

Peace

The night before he was to be tried, he slept soundly, though bound to two soldiers. Two more soldiers stood guard at the door. Every six hours the four guards were replaced by another shift, a total of four quaternions who were responsible for his incarceration.

Peter slept despite his scheduled appearance next morning before the Sanhedrin and the mob who would be yelling for his blood. Though in prison before, the experience could not have been a pleasant one for Peter. Also, he would recall that his close friend, James, had not been delivered but be-headed. (Why the Lord would let James die, then save Peter, is one of those mysteries of divine providence defying ex-planation in the here and now.)

On that crucial night the church met for an all night prayer meeting. Perhaps this accounts partly for Peter's abil-ity to sleep. Did they pray for his release? Likely, for the church depended on his bold leadership. But they prayed with half-hearted faith for they did not believe it when it happened later. Possibly they prayed for strength for him, thinking he would receive the same fate as James.

Some men the night before their execution need a drug to calm their fears. Peter had the anesthesia of heaven. He knew the God of all comfort. He knew that if the Lord wanted to release him from the jail, he had done it before and could easily do it again. He knew, too, that if execution was his lot that he would be ushered into the presence of His Master Whose risen body Peter had seen over and over again with infallible proof. He discovered that the Lord "giv-eth His beloved sleep." Peter would later write from ex-perience, "casting all your care upon him; for he careth for you" (1 Peter 5:7).

Release

Suddenly a light shone in the jail. So soundly was he sleeping that the angel had to shake Peter. Rousing the apos-tle, the angel said, "Arise up, quickly." His chains fell off his hands, releasing him undisturbed from the soldiers on either side. The angel, in effect, told him to get dressed, and to follow. Thinking he was seeing a vision, Peter fol-lowed past the two guards till they came to an iron gate, which opened of its own accord, allowing Peter to pass out into the street, whereupon the angel left him.

Anything Peter could do, the angel didn't do. What

Peter could not do, the angel did. Peter could put on his shoes and coat, and walk. So the angel didn't dress or carry Peter. But Peter couldn't knock off the chains, nor open iron gates, so the angel performed those miracles for him. God does not do for us what we can do for ourselves. A man approached George Muller, a man of great faith and prayer, asking him to pray that he might be able to rise early in the morning for a quiet time of prayer. "Young man," replied Muller, "if you will get one leg out of bed, I'll ask the Lord to help you get the other one out."

Back at the Prayer Meeting

Coming to himself, Peter realized the Lord had sent an angel to deliver him out of Herod's hand and from all the malicious expectation of the people. But now he was on his own—no angel to perform more miracles.

So where would he go? Naturally he headed for the house of Mary, Mark's mother, where many were gathered in all-night prayer. His knock was answered by the maid, Rhoda. Knowing his voice, she excitedly ran back to tell the good news to those within, thoughtlessly leaving Peter outside the gate in danger of re-arrest.

The folks within reacted, "Rhoda, you're mad!" When she insisted it was Peter, they said it was Peter's angel. How ironic! They were praying for his release, and when it happened, they didn't believe it. They were inclined to believe more in ghosts than in answered prayer. Was it their faith that got Peter out? Rather, God answered their prayer despite their unbelief.

All this time Peter kept on knocking. Finally they opened the door. In astonishment the place became a noisy hub-hub. Peter beckoned with his hand to silence their exclamations, then related how the Lord had brought him out of jail. He told them to tell all this to the brethren. Realizing he would have to flee the area if he wanted to stay alive, he went elsewhere. He didn't presume on God's goodness, reasoning, "I'll stay here at Mary's house where they know I often hang out. If I'm caught again, another angel will rescue me."

PETER'S LATER YEARS

At this point Peter drops off the pages of apostolic history, except for his testimony at the first church council at Jerusalem (Acts 15:7–11). We are dependent on inferences from isolated New Testament verses for hints as to his later whereabouts. Tradition says something about his final years and the way in which he was finally martyred.

The rest of Peter's career is wrapped in mystery. He seems to have traveled widely, taking his wife along at the expense of the churches he visited (1 Corinthians 9:5).

Probably he spent some time at Corinth, for Paul mentions a Cephas (Peter) party, though not in the least blaming Peter for any division. It is unlikely a group would develop in support of a leader who never visited in person.

Some labor was concentrated on the vast numbers of Jews scattered through Asia Minor (Turkey). He wrote his first epistle to saints of the Diaspora living specifically in Pontus, Galatia, Cappadocia, Asia, and Bithynia, provinces of an area as large as France, with 500 cities and towns in the first century. An itinerant evangelist, he remained long enough to build strong churches and shepherd the sheep and lambs.

His letters to them carry the tone of affection and intimacy. He encouraged them by his own example to endure the fiery trials they were suffering. He urged them not to fashion their lives according to their former revelings and idolatries. He knew that his imminent death—the putting off of his earthly tabernacle—would bring them much personal grief.

He penned his first epistle from Babylon (1 Peter 5:13). Was this literal or cryptic? If literal, then he actually visited Babylon where a large number of Jews had remained after the exile. Others believe Babylon was a code word for Rome, used to throw off Roman authorities from prophecies that could be possibly construed as subversive or destructive of their empire, such as "Babylon the great is fallen" (Revelation 18:2).

Tradition says Peter spent the last years of his life in Rome, dying there, reportedly as follows. Fleeing Rome because he had been warned that the authorities were going to jail him, he met Christ entering Rome. When the apostle asked, "Lord, why goest thou hither," the Lord answered, "I go to Rome to be crucified in thy place." Struck with remorse, Peter returned to the city to meet his doom. Arrested by four soldiers, he was crucified head downward. Unlike his Master he did not remain silent in suffering but delivered a discourse to his many disciples, strengthening his brethren to the very end.

The day before Jesus was crucified Peter had asked, "Lord, why cannot I follow thee now? I will lay down my life for thy sake." Jesus answered, "Whither I go, thou canst not follow me now; but thou shalt follow me afterwards."

Now Peter followed.

CHRISTIAN HERALD ASSOCIATION AND ITS MINISTRIES

CHRISTIAN HERALD ASSOCIATION, founded in 1878, publishes The Christian Herald Magazine, one of the leading interdenominational religious monthlies in America. Through its wide circulation, it brings inspiring articles and the latest news of religious developments to many families. From the magazine's pages came the initiative for CHRISTIAN HERALD CHILDREN'S HOME and THE BOWERY MISSION, two individually supported not-for-profit corporations.

CHRISTIAN HERALD CHILDREN'S HOME, established in 1894, is the name for a unique and dynamic ministry to disadvantaged children, offering hope and opportunities which would not otherwise be available for reasons of poverty and neglect. The goal is to develop each child's potential and to demonstrate Christian compassion and understanding to children in need.

Mont Lawn is a permanent camp located in Bushkill, Pennsylvania. It is the focal point of a ministry which provides a healthful "vacation with a purpose" to children who without it would be confined to the streets of the city. Up to 1000 children between the ages of 7 and 11 come to Mont Lawn each year.

Christian Herald Children's Home maintains year-round contact with children by means of an *In-City Youth Ministry.* Central to its philosophy is the belief that only through sustained relationships and demonstrated concern can individual lives be truly enriched. Special emphasis is on individual guidance, spiritual and family counseling and tutoring. This follow-up ministry to inner-city children culminates for many in financial assistance toward higher education and career counseling.

THE BOWERY MISSION, located at 227 Bowery, New York City, has since 1879 been reaching out to the lost men on the Bowery, offering them what could be their last chance to rebuild their lives. Every man is fed, clothed and ministered to. Countless numbers have entered the 90-day residential rehabilitation program at the Bowery Mission. A concentrated ministry of counseling, medical care, nutrition therapy, Bible study and Gospel services awakens a man to spiritual renewal within himself.

These ministries are supported solely by the voluntary contributions of individuals and by legacies and bequests. Contributions are tax deductible. Checks should be made out either to CHRISTIAN HERALD CHILDREN'S HOME or to THE BOWERY MISSION.

Administrative Office: 40 Overlook Drive, Chappaqua, New York 10514
Telephone: (914) 769-9000